Teen Woman's Guide

to

Life

Love

&

Career Success

*Success Principles & Success Exercises
Show You How to Be a
Superstar in Your World*

Carmen Nina Pulido

*"Success is the ability to visualize and realize your highest goals and aspirations, while loving and being kind to yourself

and others, over time"*

Carmen Nina Pulido

Copyright 2019 Carmen Nina Pulido
All rights reserved. No part of this book
may be used or reproduced in any manner
whatsoever without the written permission
of the author/ publisher. ISBN:978-0-578-54471-7
Published by Carmen N. Pulido
www.teenwomansguide.com
Contact Author via: chatwithcarmen@yahoo.com

TABLE of CONTENTS

Introduction 5

About the Author..7

Success Principle # 1 - Love Yourself & Others Properly 9

Success Exercises for Success Principle # 1 24

Success Principle # 2 - Strive for Your Highest & Best Use.........41

Success Exercises for Success Principle # 2 44

Success Principle # 3 - Take Responsibility for Your Life 49

Success Exercises for Success Principle # 3 54

Success Principle # 4 –
Goal Setting: Visualize & Articulate Your Wants & Desires.......59

Success Exercises for Success Principle # 4 65

Success Principle # 5 - Plan, Act & Manage Your Time Wisely ..69

Success Exercises for Success Principle # 5 75

Success Principle # 6 – Make "Favorable" Choices 79

Success Exercises for Success Principle # 6 85

Success Principle # 7 – Discipline & Control Yourself 93

Success Exercises for Success Principle # 7 96

Success Principle # 8 – Avoid Pitfalls & Bad Habits......................100

Success Exercises for Success Principle # 8 111

Success Principle # 9 – Appreciation & Gratitude 126

Success Exercises for Success Principle # 9 131

Success Principle # 10 – Seek Balance & Have Faith 135

Success Exercises for Success Principle # 10 141

Teen Woman's Guide to Life, Love & Career Success (TWG)

Be a Superstar in Your World!

Can a teen woman "do certain things" and "not do certain things" in order to increase her chances of having a fulfilling and personally successful life? Can a book show her how to be a Superstar in her own world? The "Teen Woman's Guide to Life, Love & Career Success says YES!

The "Teen Woman's Guide to Life, Love and Career Success" (TWG) is an interactive, age appropriate, inspirational, self-development book for young adult women who want to "live their best lives and make their dreams come true". The "Teen Woman's Guide" accomplishes this mission by offering "Success Principles" and "Success Exercises" that help each teen unlock the key to her success.

THE SUCCESS PRINCIPLES & SUCCESS EXERCISES

The ten "Success Principles" help teen women identify their strengths, talents, resources, goals and desires and the "Success Exercises" show them how to implement the Principles into their daily lives. The "Success Exercises" also help young women set goals and take specific actions that will get them from where they are now, to where they truly want to be in a month, next year and 5 years from now.

The "Success Exercises" are the key to helping teen women actualize their goals and they're also what separate this "how to succeed" book from other "how to succeed books" for teens or adults. **Teen women incorporate the Success Principles into their daily lives by completing the "Success Exercises"**.

Today, young women have more lifestyle, educational and career opportunities than ever before and while that's exciting and empowering it can also be a little overwhelming in terms of figuring out which way to go and what to focus on. The "Teen Woman's Guide" offers young adult women specific, practical, timely, life and career planning advice that will help them navigate life, love, education and career planning in the 21st century.

Check out the list of **SUCCESS PRINCIPLES** so you'll know what topics are covered in this exciting self-discovery journey:

SUCCESS PRINCIPLE # 1
LOVE YOURSELF & OTHERS PROPERLY

SUCCESS PRINCIPLE # 2
STRIVE FOR YOUR HIGHEST & BEST USE

SUCCESS PRINCIPLE # 3
TAKE FULL RESPONSIBILITY FOR EVERY ASPECT OF YOUR LIFE

SUCCESS PRINCIPLE # 4
GOAL SETTING – VISUALIZE & ARTICULATE WHAT YOU TRULY WANT

SUCCESS PRINCIPLE # 5
PLAN, ACT & MANGE YOUR TIME WISELY

SUCCESS PRINCIPLE # 6
MAKE FAVORABLE CHOICES

SUCCESS PRINCIPLE # 7
DISCIPLINE & CONTROL YOURSELF

SUCCESS PRINCIPLE # 8
AVOID PITFALLS & BAD HABITS

SUCCESS PRINCIPLE # 9
APPRECIATION & GRATITUDE

SUCCESS PRINCIPLE # 10
SEEK BALANCE & HAVE FAITH

ABOUT THE AUTHOR – Carmen Nina Pulido

Hello, I'm Carmen Nina Pulido, a writer, trainer and lifelong psychology student who's been reading and studying self-help and relationship books and theories for over three decades. I've always been fascinated by "what makes people tick" and "if you can really change your fate by following certain principles, theories or programs". Because of my love for both psychology and writing and my need "to make sense of my own life experiences" I decided to write a "how to succeed book for young adult women". Many of the lessons I've learned about life, love, success and happiness I've learned the hard way, by making one "bad personal choice" after the other and then having to find a way to overcome the bad choice and make lemonade out of lemons. I'm trying to save young women from having to learn the hard way, like I did, by giving them some "guidelines" for "what to do" and "what not to do" to be more fulfilled and personally successful in all aspects of their lives.

I'm the mother of two adult sons, but I wrote this book from the perspective of advice I'd give my daughter, if I had one, about life, love, success and the pursuit of happiness. Advice I wish my own mother had given me as an adolescent. I love my mother dearly and cherish the love and support she gave me; however, my mom never gave me any practical advice. We never talked about real feelings and issues, especially if they were negative, because my mom wasn't comfortable talking about negative feelings or negative aspects of her our personal life or history. Negative feelings and experiences were "pushed under the rug", ignored or just "accepted". The message I got from her unwillingness to address my feelings or concerns was: "what you think and feel and how people treat you doesn't matter; you're not worthy of respect and consideration, "just deal with it". This denial and lack of concern about my thoughts and feelings demolished my self-esteem and self-worth. No wonder, as a young woman, I kept attracting controlling, abusive men and I wasted decades of my life "doing what was necessary" and "people pleasing" so "I would be loved and valued". And that's why the first Success Principle is "Loving Yourself and Others, Properly".

During the unenlightened, unsuccessful part of my life I constantly asked myself "why" this or that was happening to me, as if "I" had very little control over things and was just "cursed". My search for the "why's" of my life lead me to hundreds of psychology and self-help books, to psychotherapy, church, prayer and finally to "the answers" or "Success Principles" contained in this book. These "Success Principles" were developed after much study, trial and error, self-analysis, spiritual soul searching and, finally, after much practice. Knowledge without practice doesn't produce results. Practice does make perfect!

I'm eternally grateful and indebted to the psychologists, psychiatrists, spiritualists and "regular people" who have been instrumental in helping me overcome my challenges and carve out a life that is personally fulfilling and successful. I'm particularly grateful to Dr. Phil, Iyanla Vanzant, Oprah Winfrey, Wayne Dwyer, Gary Zukav, Deepak Chopra, Anthony Robbins, Eckhart Tolle, Napoleon Hill and many of the extraordinary "regular women" in my life: my mother, grandmothers, aunts, nieces, cousins and girlfriends. All of these people, in one way or another have helped me identify and deal with "my issues." Words of wisdom from these significant others are peppered throughout this book because "all things work for good"; Romans: 8:28.

Spiritually speaking, I believe in a Higher Power or Positive Spiritual Force (PSF) that creates, protects, nourishes and guides every living thing toward the fulfillment of its own "best" destiny or purpose. I also believe that this Positive Spiritual Force allowed me to experience everything that I've experienced in my life, positive and negative, because he/she knew that I'd be compelled to "make sense of it all" and "share what I've learned". If the Success Principles and Success Exercises in this book help just one teen woman live a better, more fulfilling life, then I will have fulfilled *my* purpose and achieved "my highest and best use".

Peace and Love Forever,

Carmen Nina Pulido

Chapter One
Success Principle # 1
Love Yourself and Others *Properly*

What' Love Got to do with it?

Most of us don't feel successful because our definition of success is based on "visual" signs of success: what we wear, what we drive, where we live, how much money we have or how many people love or want us. But real success isn't about the end result or these "visual" signs of success. **Real success is about, how you feel about yourself, while you're in the process of visualizing and realizing your highest goals and aspirations.**

I'm sure Michael Jackson, Whitney Houston, Prince and a host of other "visually successful" people could all testify about external success not being all it's cracked up to be. Material things only provide short-term, temporary happiness, not long-term feelings of successfulness, fulfillment and self-worth. Long-term fulfillment and success come from activities that make you feel good about yourself, inside your mind, body and spirit, not outside of it. That's why loving yourself and others properly is the first Success Principle - because it's the most important Principle. If you don't truly embrace it, you probably won't be able to make the most out of the rest of Principles. This could impact every aspect of your life, because success happens *from the inside out*, not the other way around. Money, fame, and material possessions don't make you successful.

Your success depends more on the love, support and nourishment that you give yourself, then on anything else. If you already know and appreciate the connection between self-love and success, you're ahead of the game. But if you have *any* doubts about the importance of this Principle, or its relationship to successful living, read on.

The Self-Love, Self-Esteem and Success Connection

Self-love, self-esteem and "successful living" are intertwined. Self-Esteem **is** Self-Love and vice versa. You can't have high self-esteem, without high self-love, and the way you get and keep high self-love is to support and stand up for yourself, always, no matter what the circumstance or challenge. When you give up on yourself or allow circumstances or other people to dictate how you feel about yourself, you've already lost. Conversely, when you love and support yourself, no matter what, you've already won because you've put yourself in the right position to get or accomplish what you want to get or accomplish. Therefore, if you want to be a winner and have the successful life that the Creator intended for you to have, and that you want and deserve, you must love yourself properly, enough and always.

Let me give you another compelling reason why you must start with self-love. If you don't, whether you realize it or not, you're really sabotaging yourself, and setting yourself up to fail because you're approaching life from a position of weakness, not strength. When you make others' needs and wants more important than your own and/or you're not willing to "show up for yourself" when you need to, you're not going to get the best that life has to offer, you're going to get the leftovers; what somebody is willing to give you, what "they think" you deserve, or even worse, what nobody else really wants. Winners and successful people never settle for what someone else thinks they should have or get, they know what they want, and they go after it, no matter what.

Here's another reason why self-love is the foundation of your success plan: no other human being will ever know you like you know you. Nobody else wants or needs, exactly, what you want or need, when you want or need it. Nobody else knows what it feels like to be you or all of the circumstances that led to you being who you are, therefore nobody else can ever be as big a fan, advocate, rescuer or protector for you, as you can be for yourself, because no other human being will ever "get you" the way you "get you."

Your life is an adventure, a roller coaster ride of self-discovery, from the known to the unknown. The known is what your unique talents and skills are. The unknown is how you can best share those talents and skills with the world and ultimately achieve your "highest and best use".

While you're in the process of discovering and fulfilling your unique destiny, foes, obstacles and challenges will continuously creep into your life. Unfortunately, many times these foes, obstacles and challenges present themselves in the form of friends, lovers, husbands and family members. Negativity from these individuals can be very difficult to handle because these people are closest to us and they supposedly know us better than others, and that's why their opinion and treatment of us is so influential, and sometimes detrimental, to us. And that's exactly why it's so important for you to "show up for yourself" when others fail you.

Once you become an adult, your life is your business; it's not your parents, siblings, boyfriends, girlfriends or lover's business, it's *your* business! Stop waiting or expecting to be helped, rescued, protected, provided for, or completed in some way, by somebody else, because that's not anybody else's business - it's your business.

How to Love Yourself *Properly*

So, to sum it all up, you love yourself properly when you love, honor, nurture and show up for yourself, no matter what, despite the significant forces or others in your life who are not loving, supporting or treating you the way that they should, or the way you want or need them to. Showing up for yourself, no matter what, builds your self-confidence and self-esteem and when your self-confidence and self-esteem are high, you "feel successful" and capable of accomplishing anything and you exude positive energy that attracts exactly what you want or need to attract. That's how you make your dreams a reality, from the inside out.

How to Love Others Properly

You love others, properly, when you give them your time, attention and consideration, without causing yourself undue harm, inconvenience or sacrifice. Sounds simple and elementary, right? Then why is it so hard to do?

Why it's Hard to Love Properly

There are many personal and societal reasons why it's hard for many people, especially women, to love properly. I think the number one reason why it's hard for many of us to love properly is because at some point in our lives, in response to the negative and non-supportive experiences we've had, we forgot how completely "Divine", awesome and worthy we truly are. At some point, we started believing the negative things that people said about us. Or we spent so much time trying to prove our goodness and worthiness to others that we forgot how to think for ourselves, set our own goals and reward ourselves for our own progress, instead of basing our self-worth and self-esteem on the opinion or attention of others.

We're All Special and Worthy of the Best

Man didn't create the oceans, mountains, earth or any of the millions of unique and miraculous living creatures and things on earth, including us. An awesome, miraculous, invisible, "Positive Spiritual Force" (PSF) created everything, including us, and each one of us is as great, miraculous, Divine and as awesome, as the Positive Spiritual Force that created us. **We're born awesome, miraculous and worthy of the best that life has to offer** and as we grow and age, that fact doesn't change. What may change, due to the negative circumstances in our lives, is our faith and belief in ourselves and our worthiness to be and have the best.

When you give up on yourself it means you've forgotten how truly awesome you are. But guess what, the good news is, as soon as you recognize this and start acting accordingly, everything else in your environment will respond accordingly! When you know and believe this, you love yourself properly and you put yourself in a position to win and overcome all your obstacles and challenges.

Successful people believe in themselves first, and then enlist the resources and support they need to make their dreams a reality. Unsuccessful people don't believe in themselves or their ability to create what they want, so they wait for others to give them what they need or want or blame and resent others for not giving them what they need or want. The choice is yours, you can put yourself in a position to be successful and win or put yourself in a position to fail depending on "how you see yourself". So, commit to seeing yourself as the best thing since the microwave, computer, cell phone or whatever invention you think is really awesome and miraculous and you'll be putting yourself in the right position to succeed.

Parental Influence

Another reason why it's hard to love properly is because we're not born with that ability. The ability to love others and ourselves, *properly*, is an art that's learned, it's not something that just comes naturally. Most parents "naturally" love their children but don't necessarily know how to love themselves or their children *properly*.

Parents are flawed human beings (just like everyone else) who have reproduced another human being. And human beings who reproduce other human beings don't automatically and mysteriously lose their faults and flaws and become terrific, mature, responsible parents, who now know how to love themselves and others *properly*. Instead, what usually happens is, parents' parent the way they were parented, whether they had good role models or not. Therefore, faulty ideas and behaviors get passed on from one generation to another and children internalize bad, unloving stuff "as normal", or as what is to be expected or, worse yet, as what they deserve. Then when these children become parents, unless they're "enlightened," they repeat and pass on the same faulty thoughts and behaviors to their children, and the cycle grinds on. That's how we let the negative experiences we've had in our lives influence our ability to feel good about ourselves and others and inhibit our ability to make smart, self-affirming choices that result in successful, fulfilling lives. Negative parental role models and patterns are hard to overcome because it's difficult to admit negative things about your parents, and it's even more difficult to change negative patterns - but it **can** be done.

First, you must recognize the negative model or pattern, then you must consciously work on replacing the negative model or pattern with a positive model or pattern.

Physical abandonment and emotional abuse, by male significant others, is the negative pattern that runs in my family. I've been trying to overcome this negative pattern for most of my life. Here's how this negativity functions in my family: my mom's dad physically abandons her in childhood, and she's raised by a step-dad who is emotionally abusive. Since my mom grew up not knowing what it looked or felt like to be loved and valued properly by her dad or step-dad, she repeats the pattern and marries a man, my father, who's incapable of being there for her or for me and he abandons us via drugs and prison. Then my mom marries, a "steady-Eddie" who is physically there, but who emotionally abuses both of us.

Abandonment and emotional abuse are so damaging and hard to overcome because the message you get is "you're not good enough to be loved or valued properly". And accepting the "I'm not good enough" message produces low self-esteem, people-pleasing tendencies and "love addiction". Simply put, love addiction is when you have an insatiable need to prove your worthiness by getting and keeping love, by any means necessary. Been there, done that, lived to write this book, a novel and a screenplay about love addiction, called "Cinderella Complex".

Fast forward to today. I've been married and divorced three times because, until I recognized the pattern and shifted my point of view, I kept picking men, like my father and step-father, who weren't capable of loving me properly, either. Finally, after years of soul-searching, self-help books and therapy, I made the transition into "love addiction recovery" when I shifted my point of view from, "I'm not good enough", to "I've always been good enough, they're just not capable of loving me properly". When I made that mental shift, I showed up for myself and gave myself the love and support I needed, when I needed it. It is amazing how much this shift in perception changes your entire outlook on life.

The take away here is: identify the negative role models and patterns at work in your life and "consciously" show up for yourself by replacing the negative patterns in your life with positive ones.

At the end of this chapter you'll find a checklist of common, negative, non-loving, behavior patterns that should be eliminated from your life and replaced with positive and supportive behavior patterns.

Why it's Hard for Women to Love Themselves Properly

Another reason why many women have a hard time loving and being kind to themselves, over time, is because we're just not raised to do that or to think that way. Generally speaking, when we're still toddlers, our "girl toys" teach us to put other people's needs above our own. Via our dolls and homemaking toys we're basically trained to be "other" rather than "self-centered". And we're rewarded by those we love for this care giving, which makes it difficult to be "self-centered" and to know when we should stand up for ourselves, and when we should do what others want or need us to do.

Men, by contrast, are expected to be self-centered. And when they use their self-centeredness and self- determination to establish careers that provide for their families they're rewarded. Women, however, are generally scorned for being self-centered and rewarded for being other-centered. The thought of being self-centered is actually very negative, distasteful and "unfeminine" to a lot of women and that's why when it's time for them to make important, pivotal decisions they unconsciously choose scenarios that benefit others more than themselves because they were raised to do that. If, for whatever reason, you feel it's not right, nice or feminine, to be self-centered and to put yourself first, then you won't, and you'll go through life putting others' wants and needs ahead of your own and approaching life as a "supporting player" instead of as the "star".

The Positive Spiritual Force didn't create women to be second-class citizens. We have just as much right to be "self-centered and self-determined" as men and the sooner we realize that the better. Because, you're just not going to be as successful as you could be if you always or even generally put other people first.

Children are the Exception to the Self-Centered Rule

Granted, there are times in our lives when we must put others' needs above our own; once we bring children into the world. Children must be considered first because they're just too young, vulnerable and inexperienced to be responsible for themselves, for at least eighteen years. And the fact that children are the exception to the "put yourself first" rule is the best reason why you shouldn't have children until you have **your life** together and you're well on your way to realizing your highest goals and aspirations. Because if you have your children **before** you realize your goals and desires, you'll have to put your goals and desires on hold until you've met your children's needs, and 18 to 21 years is a long time to have to wait to get your own wants or needs met. More about this in later chapters.

Non-loving Behaviors that Masquerade as Love

And last, but not least, I think it's hard to love properly because of the many non-loving behaviors that masquerade as "love". Many wounded people (wounded in the psychological sense) have mistakenly accepted the following behaviors as part of the "loving process" because that's what they've been exposed to, or it's what they're used to, or what they think they deserve. *These are not love or loving behaviors and are usually practiced by people who don't really love you and are really trying to manipulate or control you. Don't connect the word love with any of these behaviors and don't sabotage yourself by accepting these behaviors for the sake of anything, not the children, your parents, your marriage, your relationship, your job or anything. If you do so, you're setting yourself up to fail not succeed.*

Physical Abuse of Any Kind

Physical abuse of any kind is not love, its negative reinforcement and there is just no good and loving reason for physically abusing anyone. Period. Those who abuse other people are wounded individuals who are incapable of loving themselves or others properly. And since you can't count on changing anybody but yourself, if you don't get away from whoever is abusing you, you are participating in your own demise. There is absolutely, positively, no way you will be successful or will remotely reach your highest and best potential if you allow someone to abuse you. In fact, the best way to **not be** successful is to allow anybody to physically, emotionally or mentally abuse you.

Another reason why you shouldn't accept physical abuse of any kind is because it severely damages your self- esteem and makes it impossible for you to have the confidence you need to visualize and plan for your future. So, if you want to be successful, you must not accept physical abuse of any kind!

Mental or Emotional Abuse

People who consistently neglect you, blame you, criticize you harshly, or belittle you, do not know how to love you properly and you should remove yourself from these types of people, as soon as possible. If you tolerate or accept this type of mental and emotional abuse you will damage your self-esteem and inhibit your ability to think clearly or positively. Obviously, if you can't think clearly and positively you will not be successful.

Accepting mental or emotional abuse is a sign that your self-esteem is not where it should be. Remove yourself from the source of the abuse and your self-esteem will automatically improve by 50%. Don't participate in negative self-talk about how stupid you are or were for being involved with that type of person and you'll raise your self-esteem by another 25%. Instead of belittling yourself, use the time to truthfully visualize and verbalize what you **do** really want in your life and you'll be on your way to the successful life you truly deserve.

Dishonesty

Dishonesty is another behavior that exists in many so-called "loving" relationships that should not be tolerated or accepted as love. People who truly love you and want the best for you don't lie to you. If people lie to you, they force you to make decisions based on misinformation and that's not a loving or fair thing to do. People rationalize lying by saying they "didn't want to hurt you". Many women accept lies that they know in their gut aren't true because they're not brave enough to face the truth. You'll never truly be successful if you lie to yourself or accept lies because you're not brave enough to face the truth. The truth *always* comes out eventually anyway. Lying just wastes valuable time. Example: If you're interested in a long term, committed, relationship, don't lie and say that you're not, because you're afraid you'll scare your lover off. Tell the truth and let the chips fall where they may. Keeping anything under false pretenses only prevents you from being available to get what you really want or need. It's up to you to decide if you want to waste your valuable time living a lie or you'd rather spend it being true to yourself and going after what you truly want. Being true to yourself and going after what you truly want produces high self-esteem. And people with appropriately high self-esteem make their dreams come true.

Putting Your Lover's or Spouse's Needs above Your Own

I think 80 to 90% of all women are guilty of this one. What I'm really trying to say here is **be as good to yourself as you're willing to be to your significant other and your children**. In other words, don't devalue your own wants, needs and desires for the sake of your significant others. If you're not being all that you can be, or were destined to be, you're not only cheating yourself and the world, but you're also cheating the loved ones you think you're sacrificing your life for. How can your children grow up to be all they can be if they don't see you trying to be all you can be? Martyrdom breeds resentment, anger, depression, hostility, frustration, illness, mental and/or physical disease. My mother martyred herself by staying married to a man she didn't like or love, so we could "have the finer things in life". Then she died of cancer a month before her retirement began and her husband wasn't even at her deathbed! Martyrdom doesn't help anybody, least of all the martyr. And 9 times out of 10 your husband and children won't appreciate your martyrdom anyway and will wind up looking at you as being weak, instead of as unselfish and giving. So, don't sacrifice your life for your husband or your kids. Obviously once you have kids you must provide for them until they can provide for themselves, just remember, you're as important as they are, and you deserve as much happiness and fulfillment as you want for them.

Engaging in Negative Thoughts and Self-Talk

Every action begins with a thought. Before I wrote a word of this book I said to myself, "I want to write a book that will give women some guidelines about what to do and what not to do in order to be more successful." Then I went about living my normal life, and the words came out, over time. The first draft of this book was all over the place and when I read what I'd written I thought I'd wasted a lot of time and paper. But I knew in my gut that I had something to say, so instead of telling myself, "I suck as a writer", I kept writing and focusing on my subject, instead of judging the quality of the work as it was unfolding. Different writers have different processes, what's important is that you stay positive and not let yourself indulge in negative self-talk. *If you tell yourself you can't do something, you won't be able to do it. Your thoughts are as real as anything you can see, feel or touch. Everything that was ever produced originally started as a thought in someone's brain. So be very aware of your own thoughts and, as much as humanly possible, only think positive thoughts and never down yourself.* It seems relatively harmless to say things like, "I'm an idiot", "how could I be so stupid", "my life sucks", "I can't win for losing", "boy, am I dumb", etc. But what happens is your brain accepts this information as true and then when you try to do something it remembers that you said you couldn't do it, or that you're too stupid to figure it out, so your brain doesn't try to fully engage to complete the task. But the reverse happens when you think positive. Even if you have no idea how you're going to make something happen, when you put your mind in a positive, receptive, mode ideas will come into your head and people will come into your life to help you fulfill your positive desires. This happens because positive energy really does outweigh negative energy.

In "You'll See It When You Believe It", Wayne W. Dyer puts it this way: "You cannot have a feeling without first having a thought. Your behavior is based upon your feelings, which are based upon your thoughts. So, the thing to work on is not to change your behavior, but those things inside of your consciousness that we call thoughts. Once your thoughts reflect what you genuinely want to be, the appropriate emotions and the consequent behavior will flow automatically. Believe it, and you will see it!"

Mental Reframing

The next time you hear yourself saying something negative and unloving to yourself, visualize a **BIG RED STOP SIGN and JUST STOP!** Then do what I call "mental reframing". "Mental reframing" is when you replace a negative thought, phrase or action with a positive thought, phrase or action. Example: you make a wrong turn and instead of saying to yourself, "I'm such an idiot" you say something like, "oops, wrong turn" or "this is not the way I want to be going". Take the negative, blaming, judgmental, meaning out of the phrase or action. Initially, this may seem silly or contrived but it's not. It's the way you keep yourself and your energy positive, instead of negative. It's the way you're there for yourself and supporting yourself, "in the moment, every day" instead of downing yourself and focusing on the negative.

Here are two more reasons why you should practice "mental reframing." Mental reframing will help you make the best of *all* your relationships and endeavors because you're training yourself to focus on what's positive instead of on what's negative. If you practice mental reframing with your children, husband and significant others, you won't "accidentally" mentally or emotionally abuse them by being "unconsciously" negative, demeaning, or judgmental with them. Also, by your example, you'll be teaching others to think positively, rather than negatively and isn't that a great positive pattern to pass on to your children and significant others?

How to Break the Cycle of Unloving Behaviors and Relationships?

First, you must recognize and identify the behaviors and relationships that are *not loving*. Next, forgive the people who were incapable of loving you properly. Then, connect with the Positive Spiritual Force and give yourself the love you need on a daily, weekly, monthly and yearly basis. Remember, successful living is more about how you handle and adapt to what happens to you, than what happens to you. Do things that please and truly benefit YOU, inside! Doing things that please and benefit you, internally, increases your self-knowledge, self- esteem and self-love and when your self-esteem, self-knowledge and self-love are high, you *feel* successful and you *are* successful. Consciously, stay as positive as possible, as much as possible, whatever happens, because then you put yourself in position to receive the help and support that you need.

"Mental reframing" is how to stay positive, in the moment, so restrict that you support yourself, and others, properly, daily. The more you practice mental reframing, the more automatic it will become and everybody you meet will love you for it, and you'll love what you're able to manifest.

The "Success Exercises"

To succeed at anything, you must *apply* what you learn; that's why there are "Success Exercises" at the end of each chapter. **The Success Exercises personalize the material, show you how the Success Principle operates in your life, and how to implement the Principles into your daily life**. Just reading about what you should or could do to improve your life is only half of the equation; acting upon that information is what turns thoughts and plans into reality. Getting thoughts out of your head and down on paper makes them more real than when they're just floating around in your head.

Get excited about what you'll learn about yourself while you're completing the Success Exercises! Cherish the time you spend working on yourself and your plans. The process will show you how to turn your dreams into accomplishments in all areas of your life! And revisit your Success Exercises, action plans, to-do lists and journal entries often to keep you on track and moving forward toward the fulfillment of your plans and dreams. All in all, there's everything to be gained and nothing to lose by utilizing the Success Exercises to help you clarify what's going on with you and show you how to plan the actions that will get you from where you are now, to where you want to be next month, next year, or five years from now. Once you get into the habit of being mindful of who you are, what you want and how to make plans and the take actions needed to move your life forward you'll have the life skill sets needed to live your best life and make your dreams come true for the rest of your life!

I hope that you'll share the insights, revelations and experiences that you have from the material and the Success Exercises on the Teen Woman's Guide's Website, Facebook Page and/or via Instagram videos. That way I'll know what's helped you the most and hopefully more young women will be encouraged and inspired to take their own self-discovery journey via the Teen Woman's Guide to Life, Love and Career Success. Good luck and enjoy your life's journey!

Peace & Love,

Carmen

SUCCESS PRINCIPLE # 1
LOVING YOURSELF & OTHERS PROPERLY
SUCCESS EXERCISES
SELF-ESTEEM EXERCISES

List (10) things you do that make you feel _great_ about yourself:

1. _____

2. _____

3. _____

4. _____

5. _____

6. _____

7. _____

8. _____

9. _____

10. _____

List (10) things that you do that make you feel *ashamed or disappointed* about yourself"

1. _____

2. _____

3. _____

4. _____

5. _____

6. _____

7. _____

8. _____

9. _____

10. _____

List (10) times when you did stand up for yourself when you know you should have:

1. _____

2. _____

3. _____

4. _____

5. _____

6. _____

7. _____

8. _____

9. _____

10. _____

List (10) times when you <u>didn't</u> stand up for yourself when you know you should have:

1. _____

2. _____

3. _____

4. _____

5. _____

6. _____

7. _____

8. _____

9. _____

10. _____

Forgive yourself for everything you're ashamed of and make a list called "behaviors and activities that damage my self-esteem".

Behaviors and activities that damage my self-esteem:

1. _____

2. _____

3. _____

4. _____

5. _____

6. _____

7. _____

8. _____

9. _____

10. _____

Forgive yourself for every time you didn't stand up for yourself when you should have and *"commit to standing up for yourself every time you know you should from now on"*

Parental Patterns & Influences

List (5-10) <u>positive</u> relationship patterns you picked up from each parent

Mother:

1. _____

2. _____

3. _____

4. _____

5. _____

6. _____

7. _____

8. _____

9. _____

10. _____

List (5-10) negative relationship patterns or beliefs you picked up from each parent

Mother:

1. _____

2. _____

3. _____

4. _____

5. _____

6. _____

7. _____

8. _____

9. _____

10. _____

List (5-10) positive relationship patterns you picked up from each parent

Father:

1. _____

2. _____

3. _____

4. _____

5. _____

6. _____

7. _____

8. _____

9. _____

10. _____

List (5-10) negative relationship patterns or beliefs you picked up from each parent

Father:

1. _____

2. _____

3. _____

4. _____

5. _____

6. _____

7. _____

8. _____

9. _____

10. _____

Forgive each parent for not loving "properly" and commit to not passing that same behavior pattern or belief on to your children

Make a list of behaviors that you definitely "don't" want to automatically pass on to your children

Negative Behaviors I Won't Pass on to My Children:

1. _____

2. _____

3. _____

4. _____

5. _____

6. _____

7. _____

8. _____

9. _____

10. _____

Make a list of (5) things you could do or say to each parent that would improve the relationship and/or give you peace of mind. Complete the assignment even if your parents are deceased.

Mother:

1. _____

2. _____

3. _____

4. _____

5. _____

Father:

1. _____

2. _____

3. _____

4. _____

5. _____

Love Relationship Inventory

Make a list of all of your significant others; Husband, boyfriend, children, roommate, friends or any other person who you love. Next to each person's name write all the positive things you can think of about that person and then all the negatives things you can think of.

Person's Name _____

Positive Qualities

_____
_____
_____
_____
_____
_____

Negative Qualities

_____
_____
_____
_____
_____
_____

Person's Name _____

Positive Qualities

_____
_____
_____
_____
_____
_____

Negative Qualities

_____
_____
_____
_____
_____
_____

Person's Name _____

Positive Qualities

_____
_____
_____
_____
_____
_____

Negative Qualities

_____
_____
_____
_____
_____
_____

Person's Name _____

Positive Qualities

_____
_____
_____
_____
_____
_____

Negative Qualities

_____
_____
_____
_____
_____
_____

Person's Name _____

Positive Qualities

_____
_____
_____
_____
_____
_____

Negative Qualities

_____
_____
_____
_____
_____
_____

Study your list and notice what's working and what's not working in all of your relationships. Appreciate the positives and write down some things you can do to improve the relationship(s) that need improvement.

Name: _____

What I can do to improve the relationship:

_____
_____
_____

_____

_____

_____

Name: _____

What I can do to improve the relationship:

_____

_____

_____

_____

_____

Name: _____

What I can do to improve the relationship:

_____

_____

_____

_____

Name: _____

What I can do to improve the relationship:

_____

_____

_____
_____
_____
_____

Name: _____

What I can do to improve the relationship:
_____
_____
_____
_____
_____
_____

If your improvements don't work, develop strategies for limiting the negative aspects of the relationship or eliminate the relationship altogether, if that's feasible. Relationships with minor children should not be eliminated, unless to do so is a positive for them.

Chapter Two
Success Principle # 2
Strive for Your Highest and Best Use

The term the "Highest and Best Use" is commonly used in the real estate industry. Before buying or leasing property, a vacant lot or retail space, the wise real estate developer/investor determines the properties highest *and best use*. In other words, if a space could be a shoe store, pet shop, apartment building, house or parking lot, all things considered, what would be the **best use** for the community and the developer/investor? Example: if there are already plenty of apartments, houses and retail stores in an area, but not enough parking, then "a parking lot" might be the *"highest and best"* use for that land or space.

I want you to think of your life in the same way. Based on your natural talents, your likes, dislikes and available resources, **what is your highest and best use?** Keep in mind, the world needs all types of people; people who are good with numbers, people who design things, people who entertain us, or feed us, or who take care of us, just to name a few. Everybody can't be an actress or a highly paid model, but everybody can be the best at whatever it is that interests them or at what they're "naturally" capable of being or doing. *The challenge is to discover and develop your natural talents and the skills that you enjoy using, and then share those talents and skills with as many people as possible.*

Think about it. The most successful people in the world are those people whose work impacts thousands, and even millions of people. Bill Gates, the founder and CEO of Microsoft isn't one of the wealthiest people in the world because he set out to be one of the wealthiest people in the world. He became wealthy by exploring and developing his natural curiosity and interest in math, science and technology. While he was in the process of experimenting with things he enjoyed experimenting with he created a computer operating system that controls most of the world's computers! *The point is the secret to your success lies in your ability to pursue and develop your own special interests and talents. This is true because you'll be best at and rewarded for what you're naturally capable of, or what interests or fascinates you most. Choose a career you're passionate about and the money will follow!*

Your reward and success may not happen as soon as you'd like it to happen, but it will happen. You must have faith in the process, stay positive, and know that all positive energy is rewarded, eventually. Your biggest challenge might be to stay focused and positive despite the obstacles and challenges that will come your way as you reach for your "highest and best use".

Go for The Gold!

Many people are not as successful as they could or should be simply because they don't strive for the best. Some people don't strive for the best because they grew up in impoverished circumstances or maybe they were raised by people who never encouraged them to "go for the gold". Whatever your circumstance it's imperative that you **"go for the gold"** in everything that you do because the universe fulfills *all* desires, positive or negative, therefore, isn't it better to *intend to be successful and achieve your highest and best use*, then to intend to be "average" because either way, you'll get what you intend to get. Striving for the best increases your chances of success because when you strive too low you don't have any margin for error. In other words, if you strive for the best and wind up with just "very good" that's better than striving for average and winding up with less than average, right? So always aim high!

Successful people know this "law of intention" and use this principle to their advantage. Unsuccessful people know this law too, as evidenced by the "bad luck stories" they tell over and over. If you believe you have "bad luck", you *will* have bad luck because that's what you "expect". That's why *your intention* is so important and so powerful.

Another Way to Win with the Highest and Best Use Principle

You can also use the Highest and Best Use Principle for those times in your life when you find yourself in questionable circumstances. When you find yourself participating in something that you know is bad or just doesn't feel right, whether it's a job, a personal relationship, a recreational activity or anything that just doesn't "feel right", ask yourself: is this activity getting me closer or farther away from my highest and best use? Taking drugs, being in an abusive relationship, or staying in a job that you hate is not getting you closer to your highest and best use or your best life. Surrounding yourself with people who down you or who don't have positive goals and aspirations is also not helping you be all that you can be.

Success isn't just going to fall in your lap. You have to "consciously do" and "consciously not do" certain things in order to be successful. *So, intend to be successful and increase your chances of success by focusing on your highest and best use and the activities that will help you achieve what that is for you.*

SUCCESS PRINCIPLE # 2
STRIVE FOR YOUR HIGHEST AND BEST USE
SUCCESS EXERCISES

List (5-10) of your natural talents or skills:

1. _____

2. _____

3. _____

4. _____

5. _____

6. _____

7. _____

8. _____

9. _____

10. _____

List (5 – 10) activities that you love to participate in:

1. _____

2. _____

3. _____

4. _____

5. _____

6. _____

7. _____

8. _____

9. _____

10. _____

Review both lists and list (5-10) careers where you could use the talents, skills and activities that you love to use:

1. _____

2. _____

3. _____

4. _____

5. _____

6. _____

7. _____

8. _____

9. _____

10. _____

Rewrite (5) of the careers you just listed and then write about what education, degrees or certificates you will need in order to actually work in that profession.

Career: _____

Education Needed:

_____

Career:

Education Needed:

_____

Career: _____

Education Needed:

_____

Career:

Education Needed:

_____

Career:

Education Needed:

_____

Based on your unique set of skills, talents, abilities and likes or loves, list (5) occupations that would be YOUR "HIGHEST AND BEST USE"

1. _____

2. _____

3. _____

4. _____

5. _____

Find a way to "EXPERIENCE" the careers that interest you, either as a volunteer, intern, fan or employee. Keep increasing your involvement with careers that interest you until "YOU KNOW" whether you definitely want to pursue that career or not.

Chapter Three
Success Principle # 3
Take Responsibility for Every Aspect of Your Life

Face Your Challenges & learn Your Lessons

Think of our life as comprised of destinations, roads, transportation vehicles and a driver. The "destinations" represent where you could end up (career/lifestyle). The "roads" represent all the choices you could make to get where you want to go. The transportation vehicle represents how or what resources you use to get where you want to go, and the "driver" is you!

Always Remember Who's Driving!

You are the "driver" of your life. You can steer your car/life wherever you want it to go, every day of your life! You can choose to take the freeway or the back roads. You can go north or south. You can go to the city or the country. You can go to Macy's or to Wal-Mart. Different roads and different directions take you to different places. The trick is to decide which route or direction you should take to get where you want to go. If you decide to take the freeway, don't complain about having to go fast; *you chose* to take the freeway. If you decide to take the back roads and you get lost and there's no one around to help you, don't complain, because *you chose* that route, as well.

As you drive your car/life to get where you want to go you can *choose* to take others along with you, or you can choose to take the ride alone. If you choose to take others along and they suggest or lead you in a different direction, it's up to you to *choose to* follow their lead or *choose to* stick with your own route. If you give up the driver's seat and let your passengers lead you in another direction and your car winds up in a place that's wrong for you, it's not their fault, it's your fault because *you chose* to let them take you in a different direction. It's your life and you're the driver and you choose what roads you take to get where you're going. Ultimately, you'll be responsible for where your car/life ends up, so why not **consciously** always accept full responsibility for driving your car and your life in the direction **you** want to go.

Avoid Playing the Blame Game

90% of the people in psychologists' offices and on talk shows are there to bitch and blame somebody else for their "situation". When you blame someone else for your situation you're actually saying, "I'm not responsible for my own life, somebody else is." Remember Chapter One: we're **all** flawed in some way and we don't lose our flaws when we become parents, husbands, wives, friends or significant others **unless** we, consciously, acknowledge our flaws and work on improving them. If that's the case, then it's easy to see how out of control your life could and would be if you let other people/passengers pick your destination and drive your car for you.

Other people have their own visions and goals to implement and their own issues, challenges and obstacles to overcome. So, don't give away your power, your car and your life by allowing others to drive your car and dictate the direction of your life. And don't waste your time and your life blaming other people when you follow their advice and you get a negative result. If you allow other people to drive your car or make decisions for you, it's not their fault, it's yours for allowing them to do it. Too many women blame their husbands, boyfriends, children and financial position for why they can't, couldn't or didn't do something they wanted to do. Don't be one of the 90% who spend their lives playing the blame game, be one of the 10% who drives their car/life exactly where they want to go!

Use this affirmation or write one of your own that positively states how you'll go about living your life. **Responsibility Affirmation:** *I'm ready, willing and able to be the driver of my life and I am totally capable of selecting the best roads to get me where I want to go.*

Get into the Responsibility Habit *Early*

Teenagers and women in their twenties often think they have plenty of time to be serious and focused about their lives. They think, right now, I just want to have fun! The problem with this attitude is that the careless mistakes and unfavorable choices that you make when you're young, can severely affect your ability to be all you can be in your future. Put another way, the careless, unfavorable, personal choices that you make in your twenties can severely impact the choices you make and the resources you have available to you in your thirties, forties and beyond. The fewer unfavorable choices you make in your twenties, the easier it is to be successful in your thirties and forties. So, ladies, don't take your twenties for granted. Get into the habit of taking full responsibility for your choices and choose with your highest and best use in mind, so that you're always working in your own best interest.

Your Obstacles are Your Divine Challenges, Face them and Learn Your Lessons

As you take responsibility for your life and your actions, you **will** encounter opposition to your goals and plans. That's life. Positive **and** negative energy exists in the world and negative energy will come your way, one way or another, no matter how hard you try to be positive. The trick is to really deal with the negative in a way that transforms it into something positive or something that isn't as negative as it was.

Running or escaping from your challenges only makes things worse because you're not dealing with things you're avoiding or postponing the negative or the agony. Avoiding and postponing something difficult usually only makes it "more difficult" to conquer. A simple example: you think you feel a lump in your breast, but you avoid going to the doctor because you don't want to deal with bad news. Proper response: go to the doctor, as soon as possible, so you know for sure what's going on and you can celebrate your good health and move on, or get the treatment you need, early, when it's most effective.

Average, marginally successful people dream, make plans, act and then quit or abort their plans when obstacles become too overwhelming. Anybody can quit. Winners never quit. If, after repeated tries, a winner can't reach her goal, she reinvents herself, sets new goals, makes new plans and persistently works her new plan. Remember, all positive energy will be rewarded, eventually. So, don't give up. When you're going through your challenge it doesn't feel like anything good will come of it. On the surface, it just seems like a problem, but your problems are actually "divine challenges" that force you to deal with something in your personality or your life that needs to be dealt with. **Your challenges and obstacles help you because they force you to be and do more than you ever thought you could be or do. And when you accomplish something you thought you couldn't do your self-esteem soars. And when your self-esteem is soaring you can accomplish anything you want to accomplish, one way or another.** In fact, there's no better way to increase your self-esteem by leaps and bounds than to accomplish something you thought you couldn't do. **If you can train yourself to look at your challenges and obstacles as opportunities to prove yourself and boost your self-esteem, you'll be one of the most successful people of all time!!!!!!**

If You Don't Learn Your Lessons You'll keep Attracting the Same Challenges/Problems

The most challenging aspects of your life contain your biggest lessons. **You're supposed to go through those challenges because there's something you need to learn, understand, pass on, renounce, let go of, affirm or possibly teach others to overcome.** Throughout most of my life my challenges have revolved around dealing with the negative influences and consequences of non-supportive love relationships. I kept having the same challenges because I kept replacing people instead of learning my lesson by fixing what was lacking in me. Once I began taking full responsibility for my choices and for my own happiness and direction, and I stopped expecting "love to complete me", I learned the lesson I was supposed to learn. The lesson I was supposed to learn is: I need to love and support myself, first, no matter what or who doesn't support me, because I was born worthy of the love I've always been trying to get from others. Once I finally "got that" I started to choose differently and choosing differently produced different results. Results more in line with what I truly wanted because I changed who I was. **You've got to be like what you want to attract to attach it**. Therefore, *if I wanted to have a healthy, supportive relationship, I had to start by being healthier and more supportive to myself*. After I did that, then I began attracting healthy, positively supportive people "like me".

The take-away here is: be the driver of your life and take full responsibility for giving yourself what you need to thrive. Don't let your challenges define you, inhibit you, discourage you or sidetrack you, temporarily or permanently. Face your obstacles and challenges instead of running or escaping from them because overcoming them is the way you build your self-confidence, self-esteem and your winning spirit. Once you observe yourself overcoming something difficult *you know* you can do it again, and again, if necessary. And that's a great, empowering feeling that no one can ever take away from you!

SUCCESS PRINCIPLE # 3
TAKE RESPONSIBILITY FOR EVERY ASPECT OF YOUR LIFE
SUCCESS EXERCISES

List (1-4) setbacks, roadblocks or challenges that you've experienced. Then write about what you learned or gained from that setback, roadblock or challenge:

1. SETBACK, ROADBLOCK OR CHALLENGE:

_____
_____
_____

I LEARNED:

_____
_____
_____
_____

2. SETBACK, ROADBLOCK OR CHALLENGE:

_____
_____
_____

I LEARNED:

_____

_____
_____
_____

3. SETBACK, ROADBLOCK OR CHALLENGE:

_____
_____
_____

I LEARNED:

_____
_____
_____

4. SETBACK, ROADBLOCK OR CHALLENGE:

_____
_____
_____

I LEARNED:

_____
_____
_____
_____

Name (5) things you need to take responsibility for or take control of, RIGHT NOW

1. _____

2. _____

3. _____

4. _____

5. _____

List ALL of the people you're blaming or have blamed for what's wrong with your life. Be specific and list what they did or didn't do that you think contributed to your unhappiness or lack of progress or fulfillment of your goals:

Name:

_____

What They Did:

_____
_____
_____
_____
_____

Name:
_____

What They Did:
_____
_____
_____
_____
_____

Name:
_____

What They Did:
_____
_____
_____
_____
_____

Name:
_____

What They Did:
_____

_____
_____
_____

Now, STOP BLAMING THOSE PEOPLE and list (5-10) things you can do tomorrow, next week, next month and THIS YEAR to take control and responsibility for YOUR life:

1. _____

2. _____

3. _____

4. _____

5. _____

6. _____

7. _____

8. _____

9. _____

10. _____

Chapter Four
Success Principle # 4
Goal Setting: Visualize and Honestly Articulate Your Wants & Desires

Okay, let's recap the first (3) Principles: you love yourself *properly* and know you're worthy of the best, you accept *full* responsibility for your life and your choices, and you understand that your success is linked to your ability to *visualize and realize your highest and best use.* The next step is to visualize *exactly* what you want, then honestly express your wants to as many people as possible.

To visualize means to "foresee". **You must visualize** or foresee yourself being and doing exactly what it is you want or *intend* to be or do *before* you do it. Visualization is the first step in the manifestation of anything that you desire; your education, job, relationships or Pulitzer Prize winning novel. **Everything** that's ever been produced or brought into existence began with the visualization or intention of it, first. Visualization is Point A to Point B of your success plan. **First you visualize and intend to focus your mind, body and spirit on what you want, and then you plan how to make your vision a reality.** This is one of the universal laws of manifesting and producing what you want to have in your life; you've got to *see it* before you can be it or get it.

Very few things just "pop" into existence. Our lives, careers and the fulfillment of our destinies require a series of thoughts and actions that help us evolve into what we intend to be. The connection between intention, desire and manifestation is beautifully explained by Deepak Chopra in his book entitled "The Seven Spiritual Laws of Success." According to Chopra's fifth spiritual law of success, the *Law of Intention and Desire,* "attention energizes, and intention transforms. Whatever you put your attention on will grow stronger in your life. Whatever you take your attention away from will wither, disintegrate, and disappear. Intention, on the other hand, triggers transformation of energy and information. Intention organizes its own fulfillment."

Different vocations and lifestyles require different amounts of planning, effort and mastery to be realized. Becoming a nurse requires one level of effort, becoming a doctor requires a different level of effort. However, regardless of who you are, or the level of effort required to manifest your desires, the first step in the process is the same for everyone; **visualize and intend** to be what you want to become **before** you plan and act.

Women generally have no problem visualizing themselves as wives and mothers. They want to have children because they visualize themselves with their babies long before they conceive or give birth to their children. The same principle applies to anything else you want to manifest in life. You must see yourself doing it first.

I think many women aren't as successful as they could be because they don't visualize about other things as much as they visualize about marriage and motherhood. That's unfortunate and ironic because the ability to have a good marriage and raise happy and healthy children depends on a woman's ability to meet her own needs and reach her full potential. In other words, you're not going to be the best wife or mother that you could be if you aren't at least in the process of being ***all*** that you can or want to be. No matter how much you try, you can't fool yourself or your loved ones forever. If you have two kids, a husband and a beautiful house in the suburbs, but your idea of success is traveling the world singing back-up for a blues band, you won't be the best wife and mother you could be because that's not your true vision for yourself.

Anybody can fall in love, get married and reproduce, or reproduce without getting married. Marriage and childbearing shouldn't be a life goal or career destination because it takes very little planning or preparation for either. Marriage and children should be the icing on the cake, not the cake. The cake is your life and what you make of it outside of being a wife and a mother. If you're spending most of your time visualizing about being a wife and mother, then you're putting the cart before the horse. Expand your horizons by visualizing what you'd like to be or do with your life, other than being a wife and/or a mother, first, because ***fifty percent of all*** *marriages end in divorce; therefore, if you're basing your life, happiness or successfulness on your marriage and family, you're setting yourself up to be disappointed, bitter and resentful.*

Visions That Help Many People Are Greatly Rewarded

Visions that involve helping people or making things better for many people are richly rewarded in this life and in society. Think about it: ***all extraordinarily successful people have one thing in common; they have "positively touched many people's lives".*** Deepak Chopra addresses *"The Law of Giving"* in "The Seven Spiritual Laws of Success." Chopra writes, "Practicing the *Law of Giving* is actually very simple: if you want joy, give joy to others; if you want love, learn to give love; if you want attention and appreciation, learn to give attention and appreciation; if you want material affluence, help others to become materially affluent. In fact, the easiest way to
get what you want is to help others get what they want. This principle works equally well for individuals, corporations, societies, and nations."

The following list is of people and occupations associated with successful living. After you read the name or occupation, think about the ways that each person or occupation "makes or made life better, in some way, for many people": Mark Zuckerberg, Barack Obama, , Steve Jobs, Oprah Winfrey, John F. Kennedy, Martin Luther King Jr., Dr. Phil, Thomas Edison, Benjamin Franklin, doctors, lawyers, teachers, counselors, plumbers, electricians, accountants, hair stylists, auto mechanics, nurses, artists and computer programmers, etc. Get the point. People who help other people improve their lives, somehow, make a great living for themselves and are considered very successful by society. **If you want to have an unbelievably fulfilling and successful life, visualize and focus on ways you can give lots of people more pleasure, enlightenment, comfort, security, beauty, better health or anything else that significantly improves their lives and great success will be your reward!**

Visualize Your Way to Success!

If you haven't already tried visualization, then please try it right now! Forget about your current circumstances, whatever they may be. Close your eyes and "see yourself" living your best life. See everything about it; where you'd live, what clothes you'd wear, what car you'd drive and how you'd feel while living your best life. And visualize ways that you can utilize your natural talents and abilities to improve the lives of many people because those types of visualizations are richly rewarded. Many people have become wealthy by selling ideas or visualizations that other people bring to reality or to market.

Some visions take years to bring into reality but that's okay because while you're in the process of bringing your vision into reality, one of two things will happen; you'll either enjoy what you're doing and learning, or you won't, and the universe will either support your vision or it won't. When you're engaged in something you're "meant to do," something that's true to your unique vision and your highest and best use, time flies, you're relaxed, happy and "naturally high." You also generally get support and encouragement from the universe that comes in the form of information or people who show up to encourage or help you realize your vision. But the opposite can happen as well. You can receive negative feedback from the universe. When this happens, pay attention to the responses you're getting and have the courage to dream and visualize other ways of fulfilling your destiny. Remember, winners never quit, and quitters never win!

Honestly Articulate Your Vision, Wants and Desires and Succeed or keep Quiet and be Unsuccessful and Unhappy!

Honesty is a major prerequisite for successful living. After you visualize what you want you must be able to honestly communicate your wants and desires to other people because you need other people to help make your dreams a reality.

Men are raised to be strong, independent and opinionated and women are raised to be nice, respectful, cooperative, and nurturing. I think many women have a hard time with honesty because honesty jeopardizes relationships. Some women are afraid they won't be liked, accepted, wanted or desired if they speak their minds and many women would rather be dishonest, than lose a relationship. Some women think that they'll turn people off, seem to "bitchy" or too aggressive if they say what's really on their minds. Some women spend more time thinking about what they "should say" rather than saying what they really think or feel. Dear sisters and girlfriends if you are not painfully honest about your abilities, your wants, needs, goals and your vision you will waste a lot of time and energy and you will never truly be successful because you'll be living a fantasy life not the real life you were meant to live. In *"Life Strategies"* Dr. Phil hits the nail on the head, as usual, he says, "You have to name it to claim it. Remember, the most you'll ever get is what you ask for". You must be honest with yourself and everybody else you meet about who you really are and what you really want otherwise you're just fooling yourself and everybody else. And never expect anybody to automatically know what you want or need, least of all a man, because you'll lose every time. It's a big enough challenge to get men to respond to what you *do* honestly tell them, let alone what you don't tell them.

How to Get into the Honesty Habit

If the concept of being perfectly honest is a big one for you, like I'm sure it is for many women then start with baby steps and work your way up to speaking big truths. The next time someone asks you something instead of thinking about what they probably "want to hear" or what will "sound good" make an "I" statement. "I" statements are never wrong because everybody is entitled to their opinion. Plus, the ability to make "I" statements and self-esteem are connected. People with low self-esteem don't make "I" statements because they lack the confidence to say exactly what you think or feel. So, you can work on honesty **and** self-esteem at the same time by making more "I think, and I feel" statements. And if you find yourself in a relationship or a conversation with someone who *objects* to you expressing your true thoughts and feelings, instead of changing your opinions to suit them, **think about**

changing your relationship to them.

Positive people with appropriately high self-esteem are not threatened by other people's thoughts and feelings. Spending a lot of time with people who object to the honest expression of your thoughts and feelings wastes your precious time. I'm not saying never associate with people who don't agree with you, I'm saying don't spend a lot time with people who **won't let you be you and are not really interested in finding out who you really are.** Ultimately, those types of people are probably not as spiritually or emotionally evolved as they should be, and that's why they're afraid of the truth. **People who are threatened by the truth would rather spend more time controlling you than really listening to you or helping you.**

The gist of this Success Principle is: dream your dreams, visualize your best life, and honestly share your vision with everyone you meet. When you share your vision, the universe will either support you or help guide you to another manifestation of your highest and best use.

SUCCESS PRINCIPLE # 4
GOAL SETTING:
VISUALIZE & HONESTLY ARTICULATE YOUR WANTS & DESIRES
SUCCESS EXERCISES

Close your eyes and visualize your dream lifestyle; "see" the house, neighborhood, car, clothes and family that you want to have. Now, open your eyes and write about every aspect of your dream lifestyle; be as specific as possible:

_____
_____
_____
_____
_____
_____
_____
_____
_____
_____
_____
_____
_____
_____
_____
_____
_____
_____
_____
_____
_____

Now, do the same thing for your "dream career". Close your eyes and "see yourself" doing what you think you'd be doing at your dream job/occupation. Now, open your eyes and write a paragraph about your dream career:

_____
_____
_____
_____
_____
_____
_____
_____
_____
_____
_____
_____
_____

List all the things I need to do to have my dream career:

1. _____

2. _____

3. _____

4. _____

5. _____

6. _____

7. _____

8. _____

9. _____

10. _____

List (5-10) things you can do tomorrow, next week, next month and next year that will get you closer to the dream career and lifestyle that you want:

1. _____

2. _____

3. _____

4. _____

5. _____

6. _____

7. _____

8. _____

9. _____

10. _____

Finish this sentence: I will consider myself a success when I:

_____
_____
_____
_____
_____
_____
_____
_____
_____
_____

Chapter Five
Success Principle # 5
"Plan, Act and Manage Your Time Wisely"

When you're a child your parents, relatives, teachers and social groups make plans and set goals for you. As an adult you have to set your own goals and plan for yourself. Without goals and plans it's virtually impossible to achieve extraordinary success. You may be lucky enough to stumble on a few opportunities that you didn't plan for but, eventually, your luck will run out. If you have no goals or plans you're like an airborne balloon; you'll blow wherever the wind takes you until you run into something that bursts you!

Goal setting and planning is how you move from A to B in your life and your success plan. Goals are generally divided into three timeframes; short-term, medium-term and long-term goals. Short-term goals are goals you want to accomplish within one year. Medium-term goals are goals accomplished within 1 to 5 years and long-term goals happen 5 to 10 years in the future.

Sub-Goals

All goals require sub-goals. Sub-goals are smaller, manageable, action steps that lead to the accomplishment of your short, medium and long-term goals. Your sub-goals help you break your big goals down into smaller, manageable, action steps that you can manage daily, weekly and monthly. As you accomplish your, smaller, weekly and monthly sub-goals you get closer to accomplishing your larger goals *and* you build self- confidence and self-esteem in the process. In fact, *there is no better way to boost your self-esteem and self- confidence than to set and accomplish your goals*.

Even when it looks like blessings and opportunities just fell into someone's lap, nine times out of ten that person accomplished a series of sub-goals that got them to that point; you're simply unaware of the sub-goals that lead to their current success. Example: Your friend tells you she got a scholarship to go to college. Your first thought might be, boy, isn't she lucky, when, in fact, luck had nothing to do with it. The reality is your friend accomplished a series of sub-goals that resulted in the achievement of her ultimate, medium-term goal, which was to attend college and have somebody else pay for it. The following is a list of sub-goals or "mini successes" that culminated in the accomplishment of your friend's medium-term goal of attending college on scholarship.

Your friend:

- Attended high school regularly
- Paid attention and learned her school work
- Studied and passed tests
- Got good grades
- Applied for the college entrance exam
- Studied for the college entrance exam
- Performed well on the entrance exam
- Applied to colleges
- Applied for scholarships
- Waited to here from the colleges
- **Finally** found out she'd been accepted and was being given a scholarship

If your friend hadn't accomplished all of the above short-term, sub-goals, she probably wouldn't have reached her ultimate goal. I love Dr. Phil because he cuts right to the chase, in *"Life Strategies"* he writes "Life rewards action-not intention, not insight, not wisdom, not understanding. The difference between winners and losers is that winners do things losers don't want to do. To have what you want to have, you have to do what it takes".
I'm going to add another word or trait that ALL successful people know and apply that you should add to your successful living

mindset and that's **PERSISTENCE**. You must be persistent about pursuing your goals and plans because you will definitely encounter opposition to your plans. That's just the way life is. You're only one person and you can't control everything. In fact, when you really think about it, there are very few things that are *completely* under your control, therefore, you can expect to encounter various forms of resistance during the implementation of your plans. Any number of things can happen as you implement your plans. Some people may directly oppose your plans because your plans don't fit in with their plans. Or an unexpected political, societal or natural occurrence could pop up that directly effects your plans. Or your goals and plans may need to change, slightly or drastically, based on what you discover as you implement your plans. In other words, no matter how much or how well you plan, things change, and *something* can always happen that may interrupt the completion of your plan and that's why you need to be flexible and open to developing new ways of accomplishing your goals when unexpected things "pop up." Successful people know this and that's why they have Plan B, C and D, as well as Plan A.

Talk is cheap, and excuses are just that, excuses. Don't get into the habit of making excuses for not accomplishing things and don't get into the habit of explaining why you can't accomplish something. If you can't accomplish something one-way, accomplish it another way. A failed plan doesn't make you a failure. The only way you can truly fail is if you stop setting goals, planning and acting. Remember, winners never quit, and quitters never win.

Time Management

Everybody manages time; you wouldn't be able to work, finish school or do just about anything unless you were able to manage your time. *Your life is really a long-term time management exercise that you can manage wisely or poorly.* Managing time *wisely* is a skill that all successful people have; therefore, if you want to be successful, you must manage your time wisely. Tomorrow's successes begin with how you manage today! You manage the day wisely when you do what's necessary, and you give yourself what you *really* need, daily. How do you know what's necessary? You make a prioritized to-do list or as Stephen R. Covey says in *"The Seven Habits of Highly Effective People"* you "Put First Things First". Habit Number 3 suggests that when you "Put First Things First" you are able to "say no to the unimportant, no matter how urgent, and yes to the important". Example: Your girlfriend calls to say her boss just gave her two free Lakers tickets for tonight, but you have a big report due tomorrow that you haven't finished writing yet. What do you do? You "put first things first" and complete the report and go to a Lakers game another time.

And how do you "give yourself what you *really* need, daily?" You're honest with yourself and **you do what you know you really need to do**, in the course of every day, instead of denying or avoiding your real needs and doing something else. Example: you *really* need to update your resume, so you can get a better job, but instead of updating your resume, you watch the Million Dollar Movie instead. Another example: you're in an abusive relationship, but rather than getting out, today, you deny the reality of your situation, avoid taking action and drink and cry about your situation instead.

Aside from managing each day wisely, there are certain, age-appropriate, activities and experiences that "set you up" or are "prerequisites" for future activities and experiences. When you skip these age-appropriate, prerequisite activities, you seriously affect your ability to succeed in a timely fashion. Example: getting pregnant in high school, before you obtain career skills, will seriously affect your ability to succeed in a timely fashion. In this instance, instead of being ahead of the game, you'll be playing catch up for the next decade or so.

Below is a suggested, age-appropriate, Time Management Guide. Generally, if you accomplish these milestone, prerequisite, experiences and activities during these timeframes, you're managing your time wisely and are putting yourself in position to succeed in a timely fashion.

Age-Appropriate Time Management Chart

1– 10 Years of Age: You receive love and support from your family, friends, school and social network that allows you to feel good about yourself, gain basic competencies and awareness of your unique gifts, talents and special interests, e.g., sports, art, music, science, etc.

10 – 15 Years of Age: You continue to learn, grow and manage your maturing mind and body as you experiment with hobbies, talents and interests that may become an educational or career path. During this timeframe you're ahead of the game if you volunteer, intern or work in fields that interest you.

16 – 24 Years of Age: You graduate from high school, identify career path(s) that interest you, obtain post high school education needed for your chosen career path, begin career unless Medical School, Law School or PHD level education is required.

25 – 30 Years of Age: You finish advanced degrees, establish career, travel, date and experiment with intimate/love relationships, identify the characteristics of your "soul mate", date your soul mate for at least a year, preferably two and possibly marry your soul mate. Produce offspring "if" both of you are mentally, emotionally and financially prepared to raise and support a, dependent, human being for, at least, the next 18-21 years of your life.

30 – 40 Years of Age: You continue to learn, grow, advance or change your career; make a name for yourself while managing your marriage, children, social life and need for meaning and self-actualization.

40 –50 Years of Age: You launch grown children into the world, advance your career, personal and/or legacy pursuits, travel, renew your marriage vows or begin a new relationship based on your current, mature, mental, emotional and psychological needs and enjoy grandchildren, if you have them.

50 + Years of Age: See above, plus, conquer all your demons, challenges and obstacles and be the best and happiest you that you can possibly be.

The main reason why I'm a "late-bloomer" is because I didn't manage my twenties properly and then I had a major setback in my thirties that seriously affected my mobility and options for the next decade. ***Don't make the same mistake I did by assuming that you have plenty of time to do the things you need and want to do.*** Manage your time wisely, ***today,*** and succeed sooner, rather than later.

SUCCESS PRINCIPLE # 5
PLAN, ACT & MANAGE YOUR TIME WISELY
SUCCESS EXERCISES

Write about your short-term and medium-term goals for each category below

CAREER GOALS – SHORT-TERM – (0 – 1 YEAR)

1. _____

2. _____

3. _____

4. _____

5. _____

SELF-IMPROVEMENT GOALS – SHORT-TERM – (0 - 1 YEAR)

1. _____

2. _____

3. _____

4. _____

5. _____

RELATIONSHIP GOALS – SHORT-TERM – (0-1 YEAR)

1. _____

2. _____

3. _____

4. _____

5. _____

CAREER GOALS – MEDIUM-TERM - (1-5 YEARS)

1. _____

2. _____

3. _____

4. _____

5. _____

SELF-IMPROVEMENT GOALS – MEDIUM-TERM (1-5 YEARS)

1. _____

2. _____

3. _____

4. _____

5. _____

RELATIONSHIP GOALS – MEDIUM-TERM – (1-5 YEARS)

1. _____

2. _____

3. _____

4. _____

5. _____

Buy a Month-At-A-Glance Appointment Calendar Book and set weekly "sub-goals" for each category on your SHORT-TERM GOAL

list. Accomplishing "sub-goals" leads to the accomplishment of your longer term and ultimate goals. Refer back to your Goal's List, weekly, to make sure you're doing what you need to do to turn your dreams and goals into reality on a daily, weekly and monthly basis.

Make a daily "to-do list". Prioritize your list, *"putting first things first"*. Try to accomplish everything on y o u r list every day. The great thing about a prioritized list is even if you don't accomplish everything on the list you're generally still ahead of the game because you accomplished what's "most important" to you every day. Reward yourself, weekly, for your accomplishments. If possible, get a "buddy" who also wants to accomplish things and challenge and encourage each other to set and achieve weekly goals, then celebrate or reward yourselves together.

Chapter Six
Success Principle # 6
Make "Favorable" Personal Choices

Okay, you know you're worthy of the best and you've visualized the life you want. You've also set goals and sub-goals and you understand that that your life is *your responsibility.* Now what? Now you must *consciously choose* the actions that will help you accomplish your goals. *Choices that support your self-improvement are favorable choices. Choices that don't support your self-improvement are unfavorable choices.* If you truly want to be successful you will strive to make the most favorable personal choices that you can make. That way, you put yourself in position to take advantage of all opportunities that come your way.

Generally, a Favorable Choice is One that:

- Meets a need or want (without harming you or anyone else)
- Increases your self-esteem
- Advances your goals or plans
- Gets you closer to your highest and best use

Choice, Escape or Distraction?

Choices that accomplish some or all of the above things are "favorable choices." On the other hand, choices that don't accomplish any of these things are really distractions, escapes or excuses for behaving irresponsibly. If you're honest with yourself, you know the difference. And if you continuously make choices that don't support your self-improvement you're likely to experience the consequences of an unfavorable choice.

Choices = Consequences (Cause and Effect)

Favorable choices generally produce favorable results or consequences. "Every action generates a force of energy that returns to us in like kind; what we sow is what we reap. When we choose actions that bring happiness and success to others, the fruit of our karma is happiness and success" writes Deepak Chopra in *"The Seven Spiritual Laws of Success"*. This same karmic law applies to unfavorable choices; they generally produce unfavorable results. It's up to you. You can minimize your hardships and negative consequences by consciously and carefully trying to make favorable choices or you can maximize your hardships and negative consequences by making unfavorable choices. This chapter is about giving you strategies for making more favorable than unfavorable personal choices.

Favorable Choice Technique #1: The Cost/Benefit Analysis

Before making major, costly, decisions, successful entrepreneurs and CEO's perform what's called a Cost/Benefit Analysis. Simply put, a Cost/Benefit Analysis is a method used to determine if the benefits of a particular course of action outweigh the costs associated with taking that action. It's a technique that allows you to analyze the potential pluses and minuses of a decision or action, *before* you make the decision or take the action.

Prior to expanding, downsizing, selling stock, relocating, adding or eliminating products and services, or any other "major" decision, successful entrepreneurs and CEO's **project the benefits and the costs of a decision before they make the decision. Generally, if the benefits don't justify or outweigh the cost of the action on paper, the entrepreneur or CEO won't proceed with the proposed action.**

There are many reasons why *you* should do a Cost/Benefit Analysis *before* making your major decisions, as well. One reason is, if you make a decision or a plan without analyzing the pros and cons, you might make a decision that's too optimistic, personal, costly or emotional. Major decisions shouldn't be made "emotionally" because emotions change, and tomorrow you may "feel" differently. Additionally, most every decision you will make involves other people, therefore, you should always be aware of, and try to project how your actions and decisions will impact significant others and "stakeholders" connected with your plans. Stakeholders are the people who are directly connected to, or with your plan, decision or action. Common stakeholders include your parents, spouse, significant other, children, job, boss, co-workers, institutions, companies, governmental agencies and anyone else who might impact the implementation of your plan(s). Stakeholders connected to your plans and decisions have the ability to help or hinder you from reaching your goals, therefore, their opinions and responses matter. So, when you do your Cost/Benefit Analysis be sure to factor in all of "your stakeholders".

The Easiest Way to Do a Cost/Benefit Analysis

Making a written Pros and Cons List is the easiest way to analyze and project the costs and benefits of your decisions and choices, before, you take action. Putting things in writing helps you think logically and objectively. Also, when you make a "visual list" you can easily see if your choices have more pros/benefits, or more cons/costs associated with them. The **pros** side of your list will show you the possible **positive benefits/consequences** of your choice and the **cons** side of your list will illuminate the possible **negative costs/consequences** of your plans and choices **before** you make the decision or take the action.

Most successful people agree it's much better to make mistakes on paper, rather than in real life. Granted, things can and will always pop-up that challenge the accomplishment of your goals no matter how well you plan, however, when you project possible outcomes beforehand, you're more prepared than someone who never took the time to do that.

If you get into the **habit** of making a Pros and Cons List before you make important decisions, you'll greatly increase your chances of making favorable choices that yield favorable results and consequences. Anybody can just fall out of bed and do whatever comes to mind. You're reading this book because you supposedly want to be above average and have an above average life, right? Then don't complain about how much effort you have to put into succeeding. Remember and repeat this mantra: winners do what losers won't. It's up to you. It's your choice. Which side of the equation do really want to be on?

Favorable Choice Technique # 2: Emotional Sensitivity

We all have emotions and instincts. Some of us are aware of our instincts and emotions and some of us aren't. When you're "emotionally sensitive" you're able to acknowledge the emotions you're feeling, as well as the *message* that the emotion is giving you. For instance, when you're uncomfortable about something your body reacts a certain way; maybe you perspire more, or your stomach churns or you breathe heavier. Regardless of how you express your discomfort, **the message your body is giving you** is "you're uncomfortable" and that's valuable information that you can use to help you make decisions and choices based on "how you really feel" about something. Your body doesn't lie. Intellectually, you may convince or program yourself to do something, but if you don't *really* want to do it your body will express that in some way. For example, when I'm uncomfortable or unhappy about something I sigh a lot and breathe heavily. Now that I'm *aware* that my sighing and heavy breathing is a signal that "I'm uncomfortable" I can use this information to help me decide what to do and what not to do. Another example: you're an Administrative Assistant and you're interviewing for a new position with a company you think you'd really like to work for. The person interviewing you is your potential new boss. Although the money and benefits are great, during the interview you're very uncomfortable, which you express as sweaty palms and tightness in your stomach. Intellectually, the job looks great on paper but, emotionally, something's wrong about it for you. If you're "emotionally sensitive" you'll use your sweaty palms and tight stomach as a signal that maybe you should keep looking because your gut tells you "something about this position isn't right for you".

The concept of emotional awareness and sensitivity is thoroughly and beautifully explained in Gary Zukav's book *"The Heart of the Soul"*. Gary writes, "The medicine that your life offers is your emotions. Using that medicine requires becoming intimately aware of your emotions – of the physical sensations that occur in your body and the thoughts that accompany them. In other words, paying attention to your energy system moment by moment is the healing medicine." And in *"The Seven Spiritual Laws of Success"* Deepak Chopra sums it up this way, "When you make any choice – any choice at all – you can ask yourself two things: First of all, "What are the consequences of this choice that I'm making?" In your heart you will immediately know what these are. Secondly, "Will this choice that I'm making now bring happiness to me and to those around me?" If the answer is yes, then go ahead with that choice. If the answer is no, if that choice brings distress either to you or to those around you, then don't make that choice. It's as simple as that."

The gist of what we're all saying is that your emotions supply you with valuable information that can and should be used to help you make decisions and choices. Pay attention to what you're feeling and identify the message that the feeling is giving you, then use that information to make decisions and choices that are, internally, right for you.

Favorable Choice Technique # 3: The Mastermind or Success Group

In *"Think and Grow Rich"* author Napoleon Hill encourages people who want to be successful to gather and utilize a "Mastermind Group". A Mastermind Group is a group of people who join forces to support each other and work together to accomplish something of "mutual interest and value" to all of the group members. Generally, group members have a different skill or expertise that the group can utilize to help them all succeed. All members of the group must be able to contribute **and** benefit from the groups project. Mastermind group members should meet regularly. They should also develop specific goals, plans, sub-goals and timeframes. Mastermind groups have accomplished great, seemingly impossible feats. "Think and Grow Rich" is a very stimulating and thought provoking "success bible". Buy it, read it and apply the principles and you'll be way ahead of the game.

SUCCESS PRINCIPLE # 6
MAKE FAVORABLE CHOICES
SUCCESS EXERCISES

List (5) "favorable choices" you've made in the past 6 to 12 months. Also list the favorable consequences that accompanied those choices:

Favorable Choice: _____

Favorable Consequence(s): _____
_____
_____
_____
_____

Favorable Choice: _____

Favorable Consequence(s): _____
_____
_____
_____
_____

Favorable Choice: _____

Favorable Consequence(s): _____

_____
_____
_____
_____

Favorable Choice: _____

Favorable Consequence(s): _____

_____
_____
_____
_____

Favorable Choice: _____

Favorable Consequence(s): _____

_____
_____
_____
_____

List (3) "unfavorable choices" that you've made in the last 6 to 12 months. Also list the unfavorable consequences that accompanied those choices:

Unfavorable Choice: _____

Unfavorable Consequence(s): _____
_____
_____
_____
_____

Unfavorable Choice: _____

Unfavorable Consequence(s): _____
_____
_____
_____
_____

Unfavorable Choice: _____

Unfavorable Consequence(s): _____
_____
_____
_____

List (5) "important choices" or decisions you must make within the next 6 to 12 months. Then list the "pros" and "cons" associated with each choice or decision. The choices with more "pros" than "cons" are usually the better choices. Also try to be "emotionally sensitive" or aware of how your body is processing the choices that you are making.

Choice # 1:

_____

Pro's:

_____
_____
_____
_____
_____
_____
_____

Con's:

_____
_____
_____
_____
_____
_____
_____

Choice # 2:

_____

Pro's:
_____
_____
_____
_____
_____
_____
_____

Con's:

_____
_____
_____
_____
_____
_____

Choice # 3:

_____

Pro's:

_____
_____
_____
_____
_____

_____
_____
_____

Con's:
_____
_____
_____
_____
_____
_____
_____

Choice # 4:
_____

Pro's:
_____
_____
_____
_____
_____
_____
_____

Con's:

_____

_____
_____
_____
_____
_____
_____
_____

Choice # 5:

_____

Pro's:

_____
_____
_____
_____
_____
_____
_____

Con's:

_____
_____
_____
_____
_____

_____
_____
_____

Pick at least one person you can "Mastermind" with to accomplish one or more of your goals. Make sure your Mastermind Group Partner can contribute and benefit from the partnership. Mastermind Groups should be "win/win" for all involved.

Chapter Seven
Success Principle # 7
Discipline and Control Yourself

So far, I've primarily talked about what **to do** in order to be successful. This Success Principle is about what **not to do** in order to be successful. **Not doing** certain things is as important as doing certain things because **successful people don't do certain things that unsuccessful people allow themselves to do**. For instance, taking the day off to goof off for no good reason when you're supposed to be at work or school is something you **should not do** if you want to be successful. Letting your boyfriend talk you into having unprotected sex, for whatever reason, is something you **should not do** if you want to be successful because an unwanted and unplanned pregnancy is the best way not to be successful or to make it extremely hard for you to be successful. Exercising discipline and control in your life means knowing when not to stray too far from your plan because it isn't in your best interest to do so.

A general rule of thumb for what "not to do" in order to be successful is anything that doesn't advance your plans or goals or improve your self-esteem. If you're **emotionally sensitive,** when you engage in activities that **you know** you shouldn't do, or that are bad for you, your body will let you know. Listen to your body signals and don't proceed with activities that you don't feel good about. If you ignore your intuition, body signals and common sense you'll only add new, negative, emotions like shame, regret and embarrassment to your emotional repertoire.

After you visualize what you want, develop your plans and choose the most favorable route to get where you want to go, **you must stay in control of your life by disciplining yourself not to take unnecessary sidetracks.** Many times, we really are our own worst enemies. Think about it. Unless you're truly being physically overpowered or attacked, nobody can make you do anything that you don't allow to happen, therefore, every sidetrack you take is either one you initiated or one you co-signed for. Remember if you "love yourself properly" you won't do things that you know might harm you. You're the most precious possession that you have. You're more precious than any car, job, relationship or thing you could ever have, so don't take unnecessary, unfavorable choices with your mind, body or spirit. Cars, houses, jobs and people can be replaced, but you can't be replaced. The Positive Spiritual Force (PSF) created you for a reason but it's up to you to develop yourself into what you were meant to be. Everything that happens to you can either advance or sidetrack your goals and plans. *It's up to you to choose to do what will advance your plans and goals and to choose "not to do" things that won't.* No one always chooses correctly, and your lessons are in the sidetracks and the wrong turns that you take. Your goal should be to minimize your sidetracks and lessons and maximize your favorable choices.

Some Classic "Don'ts" for Successful Living:

- Don't do things that might result in long-term or permanent consequences unless you really want that consequence. Examples: drinking and driving, unprotected sex, verbally or physically expressing your anger whenever you feel like it, hanging out with people "you know" are up to no good.

- Don't do things that lower your self-esteem. This could be any number of activities. You'll know what they are because the activity won't "feel right" or will be uncomfortable for you, somehow. Don't ignore the signals that warn you when something is not good or right for you. Just say no and do something else that does feel right.

- Don't do things that might make it harder for you to function normally. Abuse of drugs and alcohol are obvious "don'ts" that make it harder for you to function. Mismanaging your finances makes it harder for you to function normally, as well. Sometimes your "don't do" might be "don't go shopping" because you know you can't afford it.

- Don't do things that will mess up your credit or future credit worthiness. This is a big don't for young people, and especially for women for several reasons. One reason is women generally make less money than men, therefore, if you make less money, it stands to reason that you may need credit more than someone who makes more money. Another reason why women should be especially concerned about maintaining good credit is because half of all marriages end in divorce. And when divorce happens women, generally, are responsible for raising and supporting the kids on a day-to-day basis. So, who needs credit more, the ex-husband who's living alone, or the wife/mother who has to meet the day-to-day wants and needs of herself and her kids?

One of the best, as well as most challenging things about life is there are a multitude of possibilities and choices to be made in a lifetime. Just keep in mind that *sometimes what you choose "not to do" is as important as what you choose to do.*

SUCCESS PRINCIPLE # 7
DISCIPLINE & CONTROL
SUCCESS EXERCISES

List (5) bad habits, things or activities that *you know* you shouldn't be involved in or with. After each unproductive activity, list the *negative consequences* of that activity. Then, come up with 1-5 "Replacement Habits". Replacement Habits are habits or positive activities that you can substitute for the "bad habit" you need to replace with a good habit or activity.

You probably continue to participate in unproductive activities because you associate these activities with something positive and *you ignore the "negative consequences" of the activity*. If you do the reverse and remind yourself of the negative consequences of your bad habits and activities *before* you participate in that activity maybe you won't "mindlessly" participate in that activity anymore.

Bad Habit # 1: _____

Negative Consequence(s): _____

_____

_____

_____

_____

Replacement Habit(s):

_____

_____

_____

_____

Bad Habit # 2: _____

Negative Consequence(s): _____
_____
_____
_____
_____

Replacement Habit(s):
_____
_____
_____
_____
_____

Bad Habit # 3: _____

Negative Consequence(s): _____
_____
_____
_____
_____

Replacement Habit(s):
_____
_____

_____
_____
_____

Bad Habit # 4: _____

Negative Consequence(s): _____
_____
_____
_____
_____

Replacement Habit(s):
_____
_____
_____
_____

Bad Habit # 5: _____

Negative Consequence(s): _____
_____
_____
_____
_____

Replacement Habit(s):

_____
_____
_____
_____

At the end of each week, look over your "to-do" list and identify what activities you didn't complete and "why". Is it a discipline and control issue or some other issues? When you're conscious of what and why you're doing what you're doing you can *"choose"* to make more responsible choices.

NOTES:

Chapter Eight
Success Principle # 8
Avoid These Pitfalls and Bad Habits

In order to maximize your chances of being a Smart Woman who lives her best life and achieves her highest and best use you should avoid the following pitfalls, bad habits or life don'ts:

- Denial
- Procrastination
- Pre-Mature Parenthood
- Savior Seeking & The Cinderella Complex
- Escapism & Addictions

Denial

According to Author, Speaker, Life and Success Coach Extraordinaire, Anthony Robbins, virtually every action we take is taken either to: "avoid pain or experience pleasure". And, believe it or not, the desire to avoid pain is the strongest motivating factor of all. The world-renowned psychiatrist, Sigmund Freud, realized this about a hundred years ago and labeled denial and several other actions "Ego Defense Mechanisms". Simply put, "defense mechanisms" are ways that your brain distorts reality to help protect or prevent you from experiencing intense emotional pain. Freud theorized that when things happen to us that threaten our emotional and/or psychological comfort or well-being, defense mechanisms, kick in to protect, cushion and/or block our brain from experiencing too much pain. "Repression" is the defense mechanism that completely blocks the unpleasant reality. Victims of rape, incest and other horrific events sometimes "repress" or "forget" the whole painful event.

Denying the reality of their lives and fantasizing about how they want their lives to be, is a pitfall that many women fall into. Instead of facing reality, they deny reality in order to avoid experiencing the pain associated with the reality. But the problem with blocking or denying pain is that you can't block, deny or avoid the pain forever. Eventually, what you've been denying or avoiding will come to light and generally, when it does, the problem, issue or situation is worse than it was originally. Example: you suspect that your significant other is cheating on you, but the reality of that is just too painful therefore you deny that it's happening, rather than face the consequences, which might be that the relationship ends. Another example: you sense something's not right with your body, but you don't think you can handle the reality of that, so you deny what you sense and refuse to go to the doctor. Obviously, you shouldn't do that because many real-life medical conditions will not just go away and in fact they get worse if left untreated.

Nobody **wants** to experience pain, but pain is a part of life. Every living thing experiences pain. Denying and avoiding painful situations never makes the painful situation go away or get better. In fact, when you avoid your pain and your problems they generally get worse and create "new problems" in addition to the original problem. **The only thing that really makes problems, challenges or unfavorable situations better is to experience and deal with them so that you can release them in the best and most positive way that you can think of. The key is to "experience the pain so you can release the pain"**. If you don't experience it, you can't release it and if you can't release it you'll always be blocked in that area of your life and maybe several other areas as well.

Think and Analyze Your Way Through or Out of Your Problems and Challenges Instead of Denying Your Reality

Women are raised and encouraged to be emotional. Being emotional is "our gender trademark" however everything that we do, and that we are, is not good for us. Highly emotional decisions generally are not good for us, in the long run, or over time, because "after we calm down" we will see things differently. When we're "emotional" we tend to over-exaggerate reality and that's why tough decisions shouldn't be made emotionally, if you can help it, because you're not thinking as rationally or as clearly as you would be if you weren't "so emotional". I'm not saying, don't be emotional, or don't listen to your emotions, I'm saying listen to your emotions and **use your pain as a signal** to take responsible action not as an excuse to be irrational, foolishly spontaneous or irresponsible. Emotions do not have to be acted upon, in the moment. It took me a long time to realize that. Had I realized that sooner, I'd have saved myself a lot of "costly emotional decisions" that lead to costly, time- consuming, unfavorable consequences that took a huge amount of time and effort to overcome.

The tougher the reality of your situation, the more **thought verses emotion**, you should put into identifying solutions. Analyze your alternatives, weight your options and do a cost/benefit analysis **before** you take action. The main thing is don't deny what's really going on in your life in order to protect yourself from pain. The situation or pain you're trying to deny will never go away by avoiding it. Avoided pain just gets worse or morphs into something else that's even more problematic. When you avoid your pain you're actually making it more **difficult** for you to deal with.

Successful people can't afford to deny pain or reality because in order to take advantage of situations and opportunities you must analyze and deal with what's really going on. Be brave and strong enough to deal with your issues, as positively as you can, so you can release the pain of the situation and accept the challenges associated with the reality of your life/situation. Bottom line is if you're not experiencing, dealing with and releasing your pain, you're running, hiding or escaping from it in some way. And the problem with running, hiding and escaping pain and uncomfortable situations is that you have to keep running, hiding and escaping the pain, forever, and that's no way to live. So, let go and live or deny and die, inside and out.

Procrastination

Compared to denial and other obviously negative bad habits that you could have, procrastination doesn't seem all that bad. But it is. **It is that bad** because you're hurting yourself and you don't even realize it. And since you don't think you're hurting yourself or that procrastination is that bad you don't try to stop yourself from doing it. Instead you tell yourself you'll get to it *later*, next week, next month or next year, or by the time you turn 30, 40 or 50, just not right now, *later*. That's exactly why this habit *is so bad*, because when you indulge in procrastination you give yourself an excuse for not living your life to the fullest and for not being all that you can be in the present. Procrastination gives you an excuse for wasting your precious time, something you can never replace. Then, after you procrastinate and waste too much time, without accomplishing what you set out to accomplish, you feel sorry for yourself for not being the person you wanted to be.

We all think we have plenty of time to take action, but the reality is life is really very fragile and your safety, comfort, happiness and ability to act and thrive, at any point in time, is dependent upon a lot of factors that aren't within your control. Consequently, at any point in time, something could happen that seriously hampers your ability to continue on with "your plan of action" and that's why you shouldn't wait until tomorrow to accomplish something you could do today. As cold and as cynical as it may sound, tomorrow may never come. Additionally, very few things are accomplished in the course of just one or two days, however, every day, you can do something that will get you closer to accomplishing your primary goals and reaching your highest and best use.

Procrastination is also connected to pain avoidance, not necessarily intense pain, but some level of pain or irritation. You procrastinate about taking some needed action until the pain of not taking action becomes greater than the pain of taking action. Example: you have test or a report due in a week and you procrastinate about preparing for it. Procrastinating about taking action relieves the irritation/pain you feel about the activity, today, but eventually, you realize the longer you put it off, the more painful it will be to try and prepare for everything overnight. And when the pain of not taking action gets greater than the pain of taking action you take action. But why wait so long to take action and put yourself under such pressure.

Procrastination is self-sabotage and one of the surest ways "not to get what you want out of your life". Nobody else is going to make your life what you want it to be, that's your responsibility, so stop procrastinating and avoiding pain and take action instead, today, because tomorrow ain't promised!

Pre-Mature Parenthood

Women are raised and trained to fantasize about having "babies" and families, but the reality is, babies quickly grow into children and adolescents that are you're responsibly for "at least" 18 to 21 years, and usually longer. And the 18-21-year timeframe assumes you just have **one child.** The more children you have, the more years you'll spend doing for your children, first, rather than fulfilling your destiny *unless you're already financially independent before you have your child/children.* Think about it, there's no other commitment that lasts as long as parenthood. Emotionally speaking, parenthood is a *lifelong commitment* that ends when your life ends. I don't think many women project that far ahead when they think about having a "baby".

Marriages are *supposed* to last a lifetime, but we all know that they don't. And when these "lifetime marriages" end, nine times out of ten, it's the mother who winds up raising the children, by herself. The point is motherhood is a very long, expensive and labor-intensive job, therefore you owe it to yourself and your child/children, not to accept the job if you're unprepared for the responsibility.

I'm not anti-children or families but I do believe that the number one reason why most women are not as successful as they could or should be is because they put the cart before the horse by having their children **before** they have their own lives together. In fact, having children **before** you have your emotional, career and financial act together is one of the best ways to sabotage yourself and make it extremely difficult, if not virtually impossible, for you to reach your highest and best use. Then there's the maturity factor. It takes most people 18 to 24 years just to "grow up" and attain a **basic level** of independence and responsibility, therefore, if you have a baby during this "young adult" phase, how much "life wisdom" do you really have to pass on to another human being? Not much. You're still a baby yourself, in terms of what it means to be "an adult". When you have a baby before you've kicked up your heels and had some real-life experiences of your own, you can wind up resenting your little bundle of joy for preventing you from being able to do so.

Generally speaking, only the most super-organized, super-resourceful, super-motivated, "superwomen" manage to continue to pursue and accomplish their own goals **after** they start a family. Instead, most women who have children too early spend the rest of their lives trying to "squeeze in" time for themselves, and bits and pieces of their dream, until they're either too tired or too old to keep trying to pursue their dream. Many of those women wind up on talk shows and psychologists' couches whining about "not knowing themselves" or blaming others for "what they gave up" or for what "drove them to drugs and alcohol".

Money is the great equalizer and resource provider. If you have enough money you can buy the services, products and resources that you need to raise your children **and** still have the life you dreamed of.

Remember the analogy of your life as the car and you as the driver of your life/car? If so, then you should drive your car/life to career and financial independence **before** you start a family, so you won't have to spend the rest of your life playing catch up and resenting or blaming your family for **your** unfavorable choices and **your** lost opportunities.

Motherhood is the Biggest Commitment You'll Ever Make

For you "non-mommies" the next time you find yourself daydreaming about how "cute" it would be to have a baby, or to have so-and-so's baby, I want you to take a look at the chart below. Close your eyes and visualize yourself caring for someone or several dependent people for the next 18 to 21 years of your life. Note how old you'll be when you're finished your parenting job. Visualize your baby growing up and turning 2, 5, 8, 10, 12 and then 16, 17, 18, 19, 20 and 21 years of age. Think about all the breakfast, lunch and dinners you'll have to prepare, and all the different clothes sizes you'll have to buy over the next 18 years. Visualize yourself rushing home from work to pick the kids up from day care. Then picture yourself helping them with their homework, while you cook dinner, then bathing them and putting them to bed **before** you have a moment to yourself, Monday through Friday, for the next 12 or so years of your life. Be **sure** you're really **prepared** to commit that amount of time, energy and resources to the care and upbringing of another human being or several human beings at that point in your life **before** you take the motherhood plunge.

Children should be the icing on your cake. Your "cake" is your career and your financial independence. Don't fall into the biggest pitfall of all by indulging in icing before you bake your cake!

Savior Seeking and the Cinderella Complex

I think most American girls are familiar with the Cinderella **fairy tale**. Beautiful, yet socially disadvantaged, girl escapes negative and unfulfilling circumstances by meeting and marrying Prince Charming. This Girl-Meets- Prince-Charming story is so lovely and appealing, and it's been repeated in movies, on TV and in books for so long, many girls and women actually **believe** this fairy tale. Consequently, when these real-life Cinderella's meet a man who offers some aspect of this fantasy, they abandon their goals and plans, and work on bagging Prince Charming, so they can ride off into the sunset and live happily ever after. The underlying fear that this fairy tale is meant to address is that: you are powerless and can't take care of yourself. The promise or wish fulfillment beneath this fairy tale is that someone will love you, adore you, protect you and provide for you for the rest of your life. In essence that someone will "save you" or relieve you of the responsibility of your own life. When you put it like that, it sounds pretty ridiculous doesn't it? Nobody can have unconditional love and positive regard for you, at all times, in all things, and meet all of your needs for the rest of your life. And especially not someone as traditionally unemotional and non-care giving as the human male. In reality, most men are more like Homer Simpson, than Prince Charming and the sooner you recognize that the better. At least if you *expect* Homer Simpson you won't be as disappointed as if you expected Prince Charming.

When the Positive Spiritual Force (PSF) made Adam, Harry, or your Randy or Robby, he/she didn't make them responsible for "your" life. And why should he be and why would you want them to be? They're responsible for their lives and you're responsible for your life. We are all, individually, responsible for our own lives. Yes, we can come together, become a couple and even marry, but ultimately, we are all *individually* responsible for fulfilling our own needs. You shouldn't become a couple or a wife thinking that now all of your human needs will be met. There are no human saviors or Prince Charming's. Prince Charming is a "fictional" character made up for entertainment purposes only, not a person you should hope to meet someday and marry so you don't have to be responsible for yourself any more. Your first human responsibility should always be to protect and provide for yourself and your well-being. You should never abdicate that responsibility or turn it over to anybody else. To do so is to set yourself up for failure, disappointment, frustration, resentment and death, in one way or another. When you don't stand up for yourself, you die in different ways, if not physically, then emotionally, creatively or spiritually.

All of us have a reason for being, a positive reason for our existence and all of us must find out what that is for ourselves. Nobody can find or define that for us. Nobody was born to be our savior, nor should we want them to be. Smart, successful women don't expect someone to rescue them and do for them what they should be willing to do for themselves. Smart, successful women know that they're responsible for themselves and their happiness and that once they define what that is for themselves, and they commit to doing whatever it takes to fulfill that destiny, the Universe will send them the people and things they need to fulfill that destiny, not a savior. Therefore, the sooner you stop looking for Prince Charming and start **being** the Queen of your own life that you were meant to be, the sooner you'll be the successful woman that you want to be and are supposed to be.

Addictions (Dysfunctional Pleasure & Pain Avoidance Substitutes)

Remember how 99% of everything we do is either to avoid pain or obtain pleasure, well addictions are behaviors you indulge in for the same reasons; to avoid pain or seek pleasure. That's why addictions exist and why they're so powerful and hard to give up, because, on some level, all addictions "supposedly" help you meet one or both of these primary needs.

Illegal drugs, cigarettes, alcohol and obsessive food consumption are obvious addictions but work, TV, sex, abusive relationships and, believe it or not, even love, can also be very powerful addictions. The problem is addictions provide *false* pain relief and *false* pleasure/love. The addictions you choose are either in your life because they help you cover up what seems too painful for you to look at or because they entertain or pleasure you enough to help you avoid taking the responsible action that you really need to take. Addictions are really band aids that help you deny and cover up what's really going on with you. Alcohol and drugs are such powerful addictions because they help you avoid the painful aspects of your life *and* they make it seem like you're having fun while you're doing it, but avoided pain never heals, it just festers and grows larger, more distorted and harder to overcome. Smoking, drinking, having sex, taking drugs, abusing yourself or others or even being "madly in love" will never "heal" the **original wound or hurt** that caused or causes you pain. The only thing that will really heal or remove the original pain/wound is to **experience it, make peace with it and release it.** The choice is yours. You can avoid pain via dysfunctional addictions or experience it and release it.

If you truly want to live successfully, instead of engaging in addictions that cover up the pain in your life that needs your attention, be courageous enough to look for the **root** of the pain and work on healing the root of the pain/wound instead of hiding from or avoiding your real issues and concerns.

Drinking to cover up your feelings about your unfulfilling marriage will not c h a n g e or improve your marriage; dealing with the issues you're unhappy with in your marriage will **really** improve your marriage.

If your father wasn't there for you or he didn't love you the way you wanted or needed him to, going from one unfulfilling relationship to another, in search of the father you never had, will not solve your abandonment issues. The real issue beneath your abandonment issue is low self-esteem and substitutes and addictions will never increase your self-esteem or satisfy the original wound or need. In order to solve and heal your real issues and wounds, you must expose them to the light and do things that truly make you proud of yourself instead of needing validation from others in order to feel good about yourself. Talk about your wounds, write about them, heal them by replacing the time spent reliving them in your mind with new fun, uplifting, creative or really fulfilling activities that will **really** help you achieve your highest and best use. Indulging in addictions only makes things worse because you're covering up your real issues and you're adding a new problem; the addiction that you will "eventually" realize is harmful, self-destructive, non-productive and hard to overcome.

Smart women recognize the danger of managing their pain and disappointments via addictions before they get into a non-productive habit that's even harder to overcome and that will definitely not help you be successful and be all that you can be. ***Don't choose to "escape life" when the reward is in facing and overcoming your challenges."***

Addictions are Harmful and Keep You from Really Succeeding Because They Make You:

- Lie to yourself and deny your real issue(s)
- Act impulsively and compulsively for no really good reason or purpose
- Re-organize your priorities so that you put harmful, negative things before positive, helpful things
- Waste your time, energy and money on things that don't really advance your position instead of spending time, energy and money on something that will advance your position in life
- More susceptible to even more harmful consequences like very addictive drugs, jail, mental illness, disease or even death
- Ashamed of yourself for engaging in activities that are non-loving, dishonest and harmful to yourself and your loved ones

SUCCESS PRINCIPLE # 8
AVOID THESE PITFALLS & BAD HABITS
SUCCESS EXERCISES

Denial

List (5) things you're denying because these things are too painful to acknowledge. List the "pain" associated with these things and what you're afraid will happen (new pain) if you acknowledge and deal with these issues. Also list what you'll "gain" by acknowledging and dealing with these issues. Focus more on what "you'll gain" than on what you'll lose by dealing with your issues and use that knowledge to help you deal with your issues instead of avoiding them.

1. I'm denying:

   _____
   _____
   _____
   _____

   I'm avoiding the pain of:

   _____
   _____
   _____
   _____
   _____

   If I face what I'm denying, I'll gain:

   _____

_____
_____
_____
_____
_____

2. **I'm denying:**

_____
_____
_____
_____

I'm avoiding the pain of:

_____
_____
_____
_____

If I face what I'm denying, I'll gain:

_____
_____
_____
_____

_____
_____

3. I'm denying:

_____
_____
_____
_____

I'm avoiding the pain of:

_____
_____
_____
_____
_____

If I face what I'm denying, I'll gain:

_____
_____
_____
_____
_____
_____

4. I'm denying:

_____
_____
_____
_____
_____
_____

I'm avoiding the pain of:

_____
_____
_____
_____
_____
_____

If I face what I'm denying, I'll gain:

_____
_____
_____
_____
_____
_____

5. I'm denying:

_____
_____
_____
_____

I'm avoiding the pain of:

_____
_____
_____
_____
_____

If I face what I'm denying, I'll gain:

_____
_____
_____
_____
_____

Procrastination

List (5) things you've been procrastinating about. List what you lose by procrastinating about these issues. Use this list of what you're "losing" to motivate you to stop procrastinating and take action. If you do this once a week, you'll probably act more and procrastinate less.

1. I'm procrastinating about:

   _____
   _____
   _____
   _____

   What I lose by procrastinating:

   _____
   _____
   _____
   _____
   _____

2. I'm procrastinating about:

   _____
   _____
   _____
   _____

   What I lose by procrastinating:

   _____
   _____
   _____
   _____
   _____

3. I'm procrastinating about:

   _____
   _____
   _____
   _____
   _____

   What I lose by procrastinating:

   _____
   _____
   _____
   _____
   _____

4. I'm procrastinating about:

   _____
   _____
   _____
   _____
   _____

   What I lose by procrastinating:

   _____
   _____
   _____
   _____

5. I'm procrastinating about:

_____
_____
_____
_____
_____

What I lose by procrastinating:

_____
_____
_____
_____
_____

Pre-Mature Parenthood

If you haven't had children yet, write a paragraph about everything you want to accomplish or have happen *before* you have children. Do incorporate your "highest and best use career/lifestyle. Re-read and think about your "best life" often, especially when you're about to have unprotected sex with someone you're not married or deeply committed to.

Before I have children, these are the things I want to accomplish:

_____
_____
_____
_____
_____

_____

_____

_____

_____

If you've already had a child or children, write a paragraph about "your best life" and develop short- and medium-term goals and sub-goals and plans for getting as close to your best life as you can. Share your vision with your children and enlist their help; that way they become part of the "grand plan" that includes and benefits them. If your ten-year-old knows "Mommy's working on her book" as part of the family's "grand plan" maybe, she'll give you another half hour of alone time because she knows she's a part of your success plan.

Savior Seeking

List all of the men or women you've been in a relationship with or been attracted to because they triggered your "Cinderella Complex". In other words, you thought they would "complete you" or provide something for you that you didn't think you could provide for yourself. List the positive attributes that you attributed to those men, then write a positive affirmation of how you can provide that attribute for yourself. Example: JR seemed more powerful than me because he started and managed his own business. Positive affirmation: I can start and run my own business.

_____ triggered my Cinderella Complex

because:

_____

_____

_____
_____
_____
_____

But I can:

_____
_____
_____
_____
_____
_____

_____ triggered my Cinderella Complex because:

_____
_____
_____
_____
_____

But I can:

_____
_____
_____
_____
_____

_____

_____ triggered my Cinderella Complex because:

_____
_____
_____
_____
_____

But I can:

_____
_____
_____
_____
_____

_____ triggered my Cinderella Complex because:

_____
_____
_____
_____
_____

But I can:

_____
_____
_____
_____
_____
_____

Escapism

List (5) things you do to escape your responsibilities:

1.
_____

2.
_____

3.
_____

4.
_____

5.
_____

INSTEAD OF "ESCAPING" ACCOMPLISH A GOAL INSTEAD!

Addictions

List all of your addictions, the emotions or pain you're trying to cover up with the addiction and the positive activities that you could be engaging in instead of the addiction. Addictions are where you can make the most headway by simply "not doing" and not participating in that activity; it's about "self- control".

There are self-help groups for every kind of addiction, including love addiction. Google your particular addiction and you'll get all the information you need about where and when groups are held near you. Go to the meetings and your life will change dramatically because you will instantly have all the support you need from people and a structure that understands exactly what you are going through. These programs will give you tools for overcoming the addiction and people that will help you transition into recovery from your addiction.

Addiction: _____

The pain I'm trying to cover up:

_____
_____
_____
_____
_____
_____

I can do this instead of covering up my pain with this addiction:

_____
_____
_____

_____
_____

Addiction: _____

The pain I'm trying to cover up:

_____
_____
_____
_____
_____

I can do this instead of covering up my pain with this addiction:

_____
_____
_____
_____
_____

Addiction: _____

The pain I'm trying to cover up:

_____
_____
_____
_____

_____

_____

I can do this instead of covering up my pain with this addiction:

_____

_____

_____

_____

_____

Chapter Nine
Success Principle # 9
Appreciation and Gratitude

Okay, so now you have a list of things that you should think about, plan for, and "do" in order to be successful: love and support yourself always, strive for your highest and best use, take full responsibility for yourself and your actions, visualize, set goals, plan and manage your time wisely, discipline and control yourself and avoid certain pitfalls. So, what's missing? What's missing is the ability to enjoy or appreciate what you have, and be thankful for what you have, in the present, on a daily basis. Why is it important to be able to appreciate what you have and be thankful for it, because **NOBODY** *has everything they want or need, at any one point in time, therefore, if you don't have the ability to be relatively happy and thankful for what you "do have" you'll never truly be happy or successful because you'll always want something other than what you currently have.*

Bigger and better things don't equal success, advanced degrees don't equal success, a beautiful face, body or any other "thing" that you can obtain or possess doesn't equal success. Princess Diana had every "thing" anyone could imagine, but she wasn't happy. Michael Jackson had the ability to buy whatever he wanted but that obviously didn't make him happy either. All of us have things and we all want other things that we think will make us happy, but without the ability to appreciate what we have, or what we obtain, what's the point in accumulating more? There will always be something newer, shinier, brighter, more vibrant or more efficient than what you currently have, but if you allow yourself to be thrilled only by "new things" the grass will always look greener elsewhere. A century ago Benjamin Franklin wrote: "Wealth is not his that has it but his that enjoys it".

Goal setting and planning for the future is good and necessary in order to get from one point to another but, ultimately, we live our lives in the present, and the present is the only time we really "know" we have therefore, you must master the art of being reasonably happy, content and grateful for what you have now, in the present, because ***the "present" is really the only time you have to enjoy your life***. Think about it: the past is over and gone, and tomorrow isn't here yet, so when are you going to enjoy and appreciate your life if not now, in the present?

Another reason you should master enjoying your life and being thankful for it ***right now*** is because the underlying principle of all of the Success Principles is to seek and spread ***positive energy***. If you're not able to see the value, goodness or joy in what you currently have, and you're preoccupied with what you "don't have", you're focusing on the negative, not the positive. Remember the law of attraction: whatever you focus on increases, therefore you can focus on your lack and keep increasing that or focus on your abundance and keep increasing that.

Life will never be all good and perfect. If you look for the negative, you will always find it, one negative thing, person, or situation, after the other will present itself to support your theory and expectation. In other words, if you "think" your life sucks, it will suck and continue to suck! But if you try to find the good, or "some" good in everything that you have or that happens to you then, you're being and spreading positive energy and you're putting yourself in a position to receive and expand your abundance and your universe.

Why We're Not as Happy and Grateful as We Should Be

Americans live in one of the richest countries in the world, so how come we're not the world's happiest people? There are a few biological and many cultural reasons why American's are not filled with thankfulness and appreciation for what we have. The main biological reason why we don't live in a constant state of appreciation and contentment is because our brains are programmed to filter out everything that isn't new, moving or changing. Example: when we get up in the morning and are bodies are free of pain we tend to take this healthiness and comfort for granted, and only pay attention to our bodies when we're in pain and some action is needed to reduce the pain.

Culturally, as we grow older we're told to "grow up" which usually means, "stop having fun and be responsible". John-Roger and Peter McWilliams, the authors of *"Wealth 101"* credit, "Unworthiness", "The Glamour Trap" and "The Upward Mobility Treadmill" as additional reasons why we don't enjoy ourselves and appreciate what we have, in the present.

In Chapter One we spoke at length about how feelings of unworthiness develop and how those feelings prevent a person from standing up for themselves and for going after the best that life has to offer. Well, feelings of unworthiness will also prevent you from enjoying and appreciating your life. If you feel "unworthy" of life's goodies you won't allow yourself to enjoy yourself or strive for the best because you don't feel entitled to the good stuff.

"With glamour", according to "Wealth 101", "what we have is never enough. Who has time to enjoy what we've got when there's so much new, improved and popular yet to get? A close cousin to glamour (perhaps even an offspring) is upward mobility. Most of us are trained from early childhood that nothing is ever enough-there is always more to get, more to do, and we must, therefore, get it and do it. There is no time to enjoy this success-I must immediately move on to the next!"

We're supposedly more advanced than plants and animals, but unfortunately, I think a lot of times we humans use our brains to "make ourselves miserable". Plants are happy to get the sun, air and water they need, when they need it. Animals are happy to find food and shelter when they need it. Animals and plants don't "think" about what they don't have, they know what they need and go after it. And after they get what they need, they're happy, content and relaxed in the moment. Watch a dog, cat, lion, or whatever animal after they eat. They sit or lie down, rest and just "are". Take a lesson. Go after what you need, in the moment, hour and day and at the end of the day, relax your mind and body and appreciate what you have and what you've accomplished that day.

The Poor Little Rich Girl Syndrome

Beware of what I call the "Poor Little Rich Girl Syndrome". The Poor Little Rich Girl Syndrome refers to girls and women who are never satisfied with their lives and who rarely enjoy or appreciate what they have, for very long, because they're always looking for the next new, improved or trendy thing. Unfortunately, many American girls suffer from this syndrome because our society emphasizes, and to a great extent is based on, new, improved and/or trendy things. Although Poor Little Rich Girls are great for American Marketers, if you're always focused on what's new, improved or trendy, you obviously will never be happy, or content for very long, because you'll always want something else or other than what you currently have.

How to Instantly Feel Happy and Content with Your Life and Avoid Being a Poor Little Rich Girl

The next time you feel anxious, frustrated, depressed, hopeless, unfulfilled, unsuccessful and/or unhappy with your life ask yourself these questions: am I in pain, do I have a debilitating disease, do I have all my body parts and are they functional, do I have food to eat and a roof over my head? Do I have an income of any kind? Do I have any friends or family? Do I still have my right mind, relatively? If you answered yes to most or all of these questions take a moment to reflect on how truly blessed you are. And if you had to answer no to some of these questions, remember, things could be even more challenging than they are right now, couldn't they be? Things can always be worse. **At the end of every day and especially when you're focusing on what you don't have, take a moment and think about all that you do have and be thankful for it and you will receive more of what you really need. We really need much less than we want.**

We all get frustrated and have times when we feel that our lives are unrewarding. The next time you feel that way, stop what you're doing, close your eyes and visualize, or better yet, go experience nature. Look at a beautiful blue sky with big, puffy, white, cotton candy-like clouds, or sit by the unbelievably sensuous and rhythmic ocean, or look at any variety of plants and animals and marvel at the vibrancy and variety of the colors present in them, or experience the vastness and majesty of mountains, canyons, autumn leaves, sunrises and sunsets. If these things don't make you appreciate life and make you grateful to be alive then you're probably suffering from the Poor Little Rich Girl Syndrome and you need a serious attitude adjustment!

SUCCESS PRINCIPLE # 9
APPRECIATION & GRATITUDE
SUCCESS EXERCISES

Make a list of every big and little thing that you have to be thankful for:

1.

2.

3.

4.

5.

6.

7.

8.

9.

10.

11.

12.

13.

14.

15.

16.

17.

18.

19.

20.

Read the above list at least once a week and add new things every week. Keep doing this for every week of the year and you'll see just how much you have to be thankful for. You'll also see that the things you have to be thankful for greatly out number your negatives and challenges. And if they don't that means *you* are probably not taking action to change what's not working in your life.

GIVE MORE

Give more and you will get more. Instead of wanting more or something else, give more and give something else. Give a smile, a word of encouragement, a hug, a book, a supportive email or phone call. Give your loved ones more time, more patience or more help with what you know they need without expecting anything in return and watch how your gifts will be returned to you somehow; it's called karma and you are sowing what you will reap.

Record your "spontaneous gifts". This week I spontaneously gave:

1. _____

2. _____

3. _____

4. _____

5. _____

6. _____

7. _____

8. _____

9. _____

10. _____

Chapter Ten
Success Principle # 10
Seek Balance and Have Faith

Congratulations, if you've made it this far you now have nine Success Principles or tools that you can use to help you plan and act your way to the successful life that you want and deserve! The only thing that's missing now is an easy way to integrate and utilize all of the Principles on a daily, weekly, yearly and lifelong basis. *The easiest and most efficient way to integrate and utilize the Success Principles, every day, is to strive to live a "balanced life".*

Your life is "well-balanced" when you:

- Automatically give yourself what you need, and you do what's necessary, every day.

- Spend the majority of your time focusing on what **you do want** and **what you can do** to improve your life, instead of focusing on what you can't do or what you have no control over.

- Get the right amount of rest, exercise and mental stimulation, daily.

- Appreciate what's working in your life and everything that you do have to be thankful for, daily.

- Plan for the future, but live life to the fullest, today!

- Believe that you are worthy of visualizing and realizing your highest and best use.

- Have faith that, if you stay positive, the Universe/Positive Spiritual Force will help you overcome your obstacles and realize your highest dreams and aspirations, eventually.

In any given day there are a multitude of things that you could or should be doing. Sometimes you need to learn. Sometimes you need to teach. Sometimes you need to plan. Sometimes you need to act. Sometimes you need to talk. Sometimes you need to listen. Sometimes you need to confront your issues. Sometimes you need to forgive and forget. Sometimes you need to push ahead. Sometimes you need to relax and wait for results. Sometimes you need excitement. Sometimes you need relaxation and meditation. When you're not sure what you need or what you should be doing in any given moment of your life that's the perfect time to stop, get still, and meditate. By meditate, I mean, slow down, get quiet and listen to the signals that your mind, body and spirit are giving you. When you are still and quiet and you stop your worrisome internal dialogue, then you're in a position to receive the information and spiritual guidance that you need.

Emotions Are Signals, Pay Attention

Just as we were born worthy of the best that life has to offer, so too were we born with the instinctual ability to know what is best for us, in any given moment. Your body, mind and spirit are connected, and you are constantly getting information about what you "really" need, want or feel but, for a number of reasons, you ignore, deny, or tune out the signals. When you're out of balance it's because you've stopped listening to, or you've blocked, the signals your body is constantly giving you. If you make a point of listening to the signals that your body gives you, and you respond accordingly, you will always be in balance. Additionally, when you focus on **seeking balance** you will always choose the right activity, at the right time.

In *"The Heart of the Soul"*, author Gary Zukav's landmark book about emotional awareness, Gary talks about different zones of the body that emit emotional responses, what these responses mean, and how to acknowledge and experience your true emotions. Gary writes, "Each emotion is a message for you, a signal from your soul. If you do not pay attention to the signal, another will come. The message is important, and your soul will not let you forget about it. When you look at your emotions as obstacles, or experiences that you would rather have or not have, you miss the point. The point is that every emotion offers information about you that is important. When you ignore your emotions, you ignore this information."

Seek Balance

I believe addictions, disease, dysfunctional relationships, under-achievement, low self-esteem and all other undesirable physical, emotional and/or spiritual states of being can all be traced back to some form of imbalance.

A Substance Abuse Imbalance Example:

People drink and take drugs in order to escape or avoid something. Some people who drink or take drugs have trouble with real intimacy; they don't know how to really be themselves and open up to other people, so they drink, instead, in order to "loosen up" so they can be social. In this case, the root cause of the substance abuse is an "intimacy disorder or imbalance." If this person were to put energy into dealing with the intimacy issue, directly, instead of covering up the imbalance with alcohol and drugs, they would bring themselves into balance, without developing an addiction that must be overcome.

A Love Addiction/Cinderella Syndrome/Savior Seeking Imbalance

When a woman is determined to find Mr. Right and feels that her life will not be complete without him she has a self-love imbalance. Been there, done that, lived to write this book. The root cause of love addiction, Savior Seeking or the compulsive need to attach to or bond with someone else is a "self-love/self-esteem imbalance." A woman with this imbalance feels she "needs" to bond with another because she doesn't think she's enough or that she's capable of acquiring what she needs on her own. The problem with trying to fill an "internal need" with an "external substance", in this case a man or a relationship, is that you never really fill the need or the void; you just cover it up with an external substance. The only real cure for a low self-esteem imbalance is to realize that you are worthy, enough and capable of doing great things that you can be proud of, by yourself. The remedy for a self-esteem imbalance is self-love, self-nurturing, goal setting, action and accomplishment.

Withdrawal is the First Step

Whatever "external substance" it is that you're using to fill your void or imbalance; the first step in your recovery is to go through withdrawal. Withdrawal simply means: stop using what you're using to artificially correct your imbalance. Going through withdrawal allows you to experience or *feel the imbalance.* That's why withdrawal Is so unpleasant, but that's also why withdrawal is so important. When you stop using the external substance and you *go through withdrawal*, you force yourself to find other, hopefully functional, ways of filling the void or the imbalance that you have.

In my case, writing became the functional way that I dealt with my self-esteem imbalance. I used to feel sorry for myself and blame my father for his original abandonment of me, then, many years ago, just before my mother died, and after my second husband shot and killed his nephew and was sent to prison for 29 years, I started writing. When my husband and business partner left me and our two young sons to begin serving his 29-year prison sentence, I completely fell apart, internally. Externally, it looked like I was coping; I took care of the kids, sold our business, got a job, and paid the bills but, internally, my self-esteem was lower than low because I interpreted my husband's abandonment of me as validation that I wasn't worthy of having a good life or having someone who would be there for me, permanently. At the time I began seeing a therapist who suggested I keep a journal, so I could "get my feelings out." That journal turned into an autobiography that somewhere around page 50 turned into a fictional novel. Prior to that, I'd never written anything longer than a college paper. Initially, writing kept be busy and gave me something positive to think about. But once I reached 100 pages, I became excited and motivated by the challenge of it all, and by the **wonder** of the writing experience. I found that every time I sat down to write, I never knew, exactly, what my characters would say or do but if I **gave myself** the time and space to write, the words would flow out of me, miraculously. Suddenly, I was involved in a pursuit that was totally mine. Suddenly, I was doing something that made me feel good about myself and that I was proud of that didn't involve anybody else but me. I didn't know or care if I was any good at it because it just felt so good to do it. 387 pages later, I had a novel I called "*Loveline*." "*Loveline*" is a modern day, Cinderella story about a woman who transcends her checkered past and dysfunctional relationships and evolves into a self-sufficient, accomplished woman. Sound familiar?

After I finished my novel, my self-esteem rose 100%. With that personal success under my belt I decided to challenge myself again by adapting the novel into a screenplay. During that process I discovered that I love writing screenplays. You know you're doing something you're meant to do when you lose track of time and you feel "naturally high" when you're involved in that activity. That's how I felt every time I worked on the screenplay. Although I've yet to publish "*Loveline*" the novel, "*Loveline*" the screenplay, was favorably reviewed by several entertainment industry insiders and was optioned by the first producer who read it.

The "Teen Woman's Guide to Life, Love and Career Success" evolved out of my love for psychology and writing and my need to control the production and availability of my writing by "self-publishing" my own work.

I share the story of my imbalance, my challenges and what I did to overcome my challenges so that you will be encouraged to deal with your imbalances and your challenges and become the miraculously happy, fulfilled and successful person that you were born to be!

Continue to invest in yourself. Complete the Success Exercises and make self-discovery, self-improvement and self-actualization your lifelong project. You're never too old or too young to change your life!

Nothing would give me greater joy than to know that I was able to use my life experiences and writing ability to help young women live their best lives and make their dreams come true. *I know that's <u>my</u> highest and best use.* I would love to communicate with as many of my readers as possible. I wholeheartedly encourage you to write me and/or post your insights, experiences, revelations or comments about the Teen Woman's Guide on the Teen Woman's Guide's website, Facebook page and/or Instagram account. Your thoughts and insights will help me know what you found most valuable and hopefully will encourage other young women to be a part of a mass movement of women determined to "live their best lives" and "make their dreams come true". You only have one life! Live it as joyfully and successfully as possible!

Eternal Peace, Love & Respect,

Carmen Nina Pulido

SUCCESS PRINCIPLE # 10
SEEK BALANCE
SUCCESS EXERCISES

List the ways you know your life is out of balance. Example: you know you don't get enough sleep, exercise, social interactions or healthy food and that these things are negatively impacting your overall well-being.

Imbalance:

_____

Corrective Activity:

_____

Imbalance:

_____

Corrective Activity:

_____

Imbalance:

_____

Corrective Activity:

_____

Imbalance:

_____

Corrective Activity:

_____

Imbalance:

_____

Corrective Activity:

_____

Commit to correcting your imbalances, if not all at once, slowly but surely, one bad habit at a time. And if you have children, look for, identify and seek to remedy imbalances you notice in them *before* those imbalances become lifelong bad habits or they lead to worse habits or addictions.

Live your life as "consciously" or as "mindful" as possible. Don't "ignore" the signals and messages that your body, mind, spirit and life experiences are constantly giving you. Respond to the messages by giving yourself what you need, when you need it, daily, weekly, monthly and yearly, for the rest of your life. Make a list of "everything that you can think of that makes you feel good, healthy, happy, relaxed, proud or comfortable. Then make a point of doing as many of those things as possible, on a daily basis. When you are bored, anxious or depressed, look at this list and do some of the things on it!

Things I love to do or experience:

1. _____

2. _____

3. _____

4. _____

5. _____

6. _____

7. _____

8. _____

9. _____

10. _____

And last but not least, ENJOY YOUR LIFE EVERY SINGLE DAY - YOU DESERVE IT!

Peace and Love Eternally,

Carmen Nina Pulido

www.ingramcontent.com/pod-product-compliance
Lightning Source LLC
Chambersburg PA
CBHW071403290426
44108CB00014B/1671